THE FUTURE OF
FOOTBALL

CZONKO BEZRSKI, JR.

ISBN: 978-1-68222-054-2

TABLE OF CONTENTS

PREFACE   vii

INTRO   ix

Chapter 1 – Outside of the Pocket   1

Chapter 2 – Scatback-Quarterback   15

Chapter 3 – Kid's Play   27

Chapter 4 – Grit & Grind   41

Chapter 5 – Perks of the Game   57

Chapter 6 – Straight & Narrow   71

Chapter 7 – Tug of War   89

Chapter 8 – Save the Day   105

Chapter 9 – Come What May   125

Chapter 10 – Don't Look Back   145

OUTRO   156

FUMBLEGATE: *The Cover-up*   160

PREFACE

Thank you to my new friends with Smith Publicity and BookBaby who worked to bring this book to print, and *print-edition* eBook. It has been such a privilege to work with you.

To Dan Smith, Sandy Poirier Smith, Corinne Liccketto, Mallory Campoli, Kathy Weick and Naz Hashmi… Thank you all over again, for your professionalism as publicist for this book. It has been an honor, as much as it has been fun. I've been impressed and blessed to have such a gifted team of insightful talents to work with.

And to the good hearts at BookBaby who introduced me to you. Special thanks, in your respective areas of expertise, to: Crystal, Technical Specialist; Maddie, Nikola, Jessica and Stacey, eBook team; Lori and John Morad, Print team.

The term "self-publishing" has a lot less to do with SELF, and a lot more to do with TEAM, I've learned. Thank you to the great team of team-players for all the teamwork it took. To make this book a reality.

INTRO

The NFL gladiators competing in new age arenas these days, pretty much all started playing as a kid under the age of 13. Something athletes around the world share in common with each other. They all started as a kid.

For today's NFL stars it was running, kicking, hitting, blocking, throwing, catching and playing as a kid first. And that's what's fun. The intrinsic nature of the game is playing for fun, and that brings the kid out in us.

When my dad was a kid they didn't wear facemasks. But he navigated his career without a single major injury. Some players are blessed like that. I had my dad's bloodline, so the magic was there: Will force and raw talent... But my intangible combination of cat-like quickness and pure speed made me a phenomenon to see as a young football player.

Quarterback / Tailback / Cornerback / Safety / Kick and Punt Returner... All of the above were my positions. And people who saw the spectacle of my play have reminded me how fun it was to watch. That's humbling considering I didn't play long.

Dad coached me in elementary school, and he was a tough old character. I still remember running to catch a pass on a long route after practice with the other kids watching. I thought I'd be making an incredible catch in front of them all. But the pass sent me into the path of the wooden goal posts in the end zone. Running as fast as I could, I reached out to catch the ball... Right hand just to the right of the goal post, left hand just to the left, I was looking back at the ball coming down...

The next instant: **WHAM!**

My whole body hit the wooden post square and it didn't budge. I bounced off cold-cocked and fell to the ground. The world spinning around and the wind knocked out of me, I couldn't breathe. But heard dad holler, "CATCH THE BALL!" I twisted over and under, then back around to look upside-down at the other end of the field. The kids were all laughing. My helmet was crooked. It must have looked funny.

But most of my youth sports life was just the opposite. I was a living highlight reel. It was a blast playing like I played, and fun to watch for fans. I don't remember ever playing a grade school game I didn't score at least one touchdown. I actually can't remember a game I didn't score twice. Sometimes on defense, sometimes on offense or on kick or punt returns. It was so fun playing like that. Being a playmaker making plays.

I had the quickness and speed everybody wanted naturally. I was born with it. Didn't have to work or struggle for it. My dad said it all came too easy for me. He had to work harder for his success. Mine was pure gift, he said. But in reality I did work hard to improve and be my best.

Before my 5th grade season the other team's coaches got together and demanded a new rule to slow me down after my 4th grade romp. The rule was meant to stop me specifically, from running wild. I was the spirited running quarterback nobody could handle. And nobody else played like us, so it was only going to affect our team. The other coaches pressed and the league caved to the pressure, creating a special rule to make me one-dimensional. So I had to play like the other quarterbacks played.

According to the new rule, no player taking the snap could run with the ball. That was the whole rule. Unbelievable! You had to pitch the ball or pass, but you could not run if you took the snap from center. That was a huge part of my game, taking the snap and running or passing. It made me furious they would create a rule just to stop me. But dad said, "Don't worry son."

Then he drew up some new schemes to beat the rule where we had two quarterback playmakers sharing the ball in the backfield instead of one. Wonderful idea! The perfect way to get around that rule. We would snap the ball to our new co-quarterback and he would pitch to me. That way I could run or pass again, and nobody could stop me.

Dad retooled our plays so we had a multi-faceted very original offense. The ball would be snapped to one of our two quarterbacks, but not always the same one. When we wanted a run-throw option, it was snapped to the other quarterback who pitched it to me. Kind of convoluted, but it worked.

We developed our offense around this dual quarterback game to get around the rule. He pitched to me 70% of the time, but didn't always pitch to me. Sometimes he passed the ball or handed off to our other backs. It proved quite unstoppable, as teams never knew what to expect.

I had an indomitable will to make plays for my team, but I didn't last long in the game. I flamed out too early for a natural talent. Why have people heard of my dad, and not me? What could have happened to waylay a great football talent like I was in my youthful prime? The same thing that takes most players sooner or later...

Wear and tear... Injuries. Mine just happened to be severe and consecutive.

Yep, in high school I had back-to-back Spring Training injuries and back-to-back summer surgeries that cut short a great thing. What luck! The good thing is, I got to experience what its like playing football with extraordinary quickness and speed, and I got to play multi-threat quarterback. Yes, and amen! The way the game should be played in my opinion. By chance, I also got the privilege to play in a backfield with two quarterbacks instead of one, and learned how well it works.

I would love to see the NFL game played like I played when I was a kid.

Being a great open field runner gives a quarterback a huge advantage. Right when the defense thinks you're passing, you can run up field for big gains. Right when they think you're running, you can pull back and pass to a wide-open receiver. If you have the quickness, it's easy to create the opportunities to break free. If you have the speed and you do break into the clear, nobody can catch you.

Let the playmakers make plays is what I say. Yes, and amen!

After thinking about it, and watching how the game is trending. I can tell you the NFL game is flirting with the idea big time! Yes, a new style of offensive play is about to take over. A new style quarterback and offensive play is coming to transform the NFL game. The revamping of the quarterback position will continue to unfold, and the quarterback role, continue to evolve. **Today's defenses are forcing it.**

The quarterback role must transform into something new. It has to...

The multi-threat quarterback has to take over. The historic drop back pocket passer must be replaced. And here's the biggest change that must come to allow this. The new multi-skilled quarterbacks must get new playbooks designed around their specific skills, so they aren't forced to fit into old playbooks for drop back pocket passers.

Imagine Tom Brady calling plays from a multi-threat playbook that requires him to rush the ball? Or Eli Manning, operating from a multi-threat playbook where he has to run too... It wouldn't work. Drop back pocket passers dominate the game solely because their style-of-playbook rules. Though that is changing. With the defenses forcing it, like happened to Eli in his record 5-interception performance versus the future-threatening San Francisco 49ers.

Which is why I believe I'm predicting the obvious.

New playbooks designed for new multi-skilled quarterbacks will eventually rule in the NFL as more multi-threat playmakers take over from traditional one-dimensional drop back pocket passers who can't effectively run the ball too.

Don't think so?

1

OUTSIDE OF THE POCKET

Have we already seen a glimpse of the future? Has the progression of the NFL game given us a snapshot of The Future of Football? Because we've seen a running quarterback competing in the Super Bowl the past 3-years in a row!

Was it a trending reality we saw back in 2014, in the NFC Championship game? With running quarterback Colin Kaepernick pitched against running quarterback Russell Wilson. The playoff game of the year that was so much more competitive and entertaining than the runaway Seattle Super Bowl victory against Denver.

Looking back, I would venture to say yes. We saw a new reality when Wilson and Kaepernick squared off in that game. And in the 2014 Super Bowl with multi-threat quarterback Russell Wilson dominating Denver's one-dimensional Peyton Manning. Nothing against Manning since his 2013/2014 stats speak for themselves. On the technical side that is, looking at his numbers, Manning had an extraordinary year leading the Broncos to the Super Bowl.

So, how was Manning's offense so completely dismantled in the big game? The answer to that question points to where the NFL game is trending and why. Because there is a simple reason why the game is trending where it is trending.

Manning was undone in the Super Bowl by mere split seconds. Almost no time at all. Not full seconds, but split seconds. Seattle pressured Manning just barely enough to make his "time to throw" shorter than normal by fractions of a second. How simple is that? Russell Wilson meanwhile, was able to stretch out his "time to throw" by not always staying in the pocket, and at key times running the ball to pick up critical first down yardage to keep scoring drives alive.

The Seattle Seahawks gave us a peek into the future rallying around a defense that took fractions of a second from Denver's drop back pocket passer's time to throw. While their own multi-threat quarterback was leading the Seahawks with just enough passing yards combined with just enough critical rushing yards on three scrambles.

That was the difference in the game. Signed, sealed, delivered...

When Seattle needed someone to turn a broken play into something more, Wilson was there to deliver with his running. Didn't happen often in the Super Bowl, but it did happen, and he stretched out his own time to throw by moving around in, and outside of the pocket.

On one second-half play the Broncos needed to hold Wilson on 3rd and 10. The play started as a pass. Denver defended it so perfectly there was nowhere to throw the ball. Everybody was covered and the rush was pressuring Wilson... Not a problem, but an opportunity for the multi-threat playmaker who dashed downfield for the first down.

Manning, in the traditional drop back pocket-passing role was at a disadvantage against the league's quickest defense ever. And there was an easy way to look at this and see why what happened in the Super Bowl makes sense.

Just compare the "time to throw" of the two quarterbacks by their average time to throw stats provided in the timely ProFootballFocus.com article titled, "Signature Stat Snapshot: Time to Throw." It's dumb simple. Russell Wilson rated #1 in time to throw with an average of 3.14-seconds. Manning rated #31 of 33 teams, with a 2.51-second time to throw. How interesting... The one statistical reality that underlies what is trending in the NFL today.

Let's break it down...

Wilson's 3.14-seconds minus Manning's 2.51-seconds equals a difference of .63-seconds, which is more than a half second. Manning was at a disadvantage in his time to throw alone. But it gets worse.

The "time to sack" for each quarterback in the article had Wilson again at #1, with a 4.05-second average time before getting sacked, and Manning close to last at #30, with almost the same time to sack, as time to throw. Wilson had the clear advantage with almost a full second between his 3.14-second time to pass, and 4.05-second time to sack.

What a difference a slice of time can make in a game of inches.

Force Manning into anything less than his tight time to throw and he's sacked. Just the opposite for Wilson with his ability to move in the traditional pocket, or roam about in a moving pocket, or run the ball downfield. If this held up exactly in the Super Bowl, which it appeared to do, Wilson averaged close to 1-full second longer to pass than Manning, per passing play.

If you saw the game, you saw the defense take split seconds from Manning's timing, reducing his passing efficiency by rushed throws, two interceptions and other near interceptions. The quickest defense in the league was too quick for the best drop back pocket passing elite champion quarterback who can't run the ball. Though a phenomenal leader he is not a runner.

The future demands offenses improve in how they respond to the quickest defenses in football history, as more teams improve and the game continues to grow and transition. We all have to remember sports records are meant to be broken. So, the future will not allow athletes or coaches to "rest on their laurels" and be happy with past achievements without doing anything to improve. That is not how it works.

The future demands better, greater, higher, faster, stronger, quicker... That is how the future works. Can you look back in the past and find better statistics going back in time in any sport?

In pro football the multi-threat quarterback of today's game is the precursor model to the "multi-threat backfields" coming in the future. The game is transitioning in this direction without anyone's approval or consent. Get used to it or go suck an egg. A new shift in the quarterback role and new style of play is coming to a team near you: SOON!

It won't stop trending in this direction for the sake of slow minds trapped in old models. No matter what the old model can do, the new model can do better. Before the 2014 Super Bowl, a story ran in the Bleacher Report titled: "Why Russell Wilson Will Be Seattle Seahawks' Downfall in the Super Bowl."

Ha! Say WHAT? How funny that sounds now... The tin soldier quarterback role is a fading model, though it remains part of today's NFL game.

We're always stuck in the present, because the past is behind us and the future never gets here, right? Wrong.

Pro playbooks designed for one-dimensional drop-back pocket passers keep the old-style quarterbacks looking like they're the best in the game. But things have been changing in recent years as some playbooks have begun to morph towards the playmaking abilities of multi-threat playmakers. Old offensive schemes created for one-dimensional quarterbacks will not work for the new multi-threat backfields of the future.

The present can only stick around for as long as it takes someone like Pete Carroll to fill his roster with multi-threat playmakers at the quarterback position, as he has done. And once that happens for more teams in the league, which is happening btw, the future will be here to stay. Not waiting for your consent.

Here's another prediction: In the future more playmakers will take snaps than just one over-emphasized one-dimensional guy. The role of quarterback will evolve and change as it keeps pace with today's quicker faster athletes who are playing the game like it has never been played. It is inevitable. The running passer multi-threat playmaker model will keep developing right before our eyes.

Watch and see... This trend is unfolding... Multi-threat playmaker-QB Colin Kaepernick almost came from behind to win a Super Bowl. The next year, multi-threat playmaker-QB Russell Wilson did lead his team to a Super Bowl victory. And Wilson almost won back-to-back Super Bowls, save only for one of the worst play call in Super Bowl history.

I had the good fortune to try this theory on a small scale in a youth sports setting. Since I was the coach I could do whatever I wanted, and I wanted to try it. So my football teams had several x3 multi-threat playmakers share in taking the snaps.

The plays we ran were designed around this premise. Together the three of them were our collective quarterback and more. This stopped the over emphasis of a single player, so no team could knock our starting quarterback out of the game. We didn't have one. We had a unit of three playmakers who shared the roles of running quarterback, passer and receiver.

The NFL will see this model take over someday.

A wonderfully prophetic article from the New York Daily News 2014-February 1, described this multi-threat quarterback model perfectly. When Ebenezer Samuel absolutely nailed what is trending today.

Whether the football God was speaking through Samuel as a real prophet or not... The man could not have given a more accurate account of the pivotal transition the NFL quarterback position is going through right now.

EXCERPTS FROM:

Super Bowl XLVIII: Russell Wilson is the man on the run

By Ebenezer Samuel

NEW YORK DAILY NEWS / February 2014

No matter what happens Sunday, Russell Wilson has made history. The Seahawks QB rushed for 539 yards this season, the most by any quarterback to play for the title in the Super Bowl era.

Carl Smith used to cringe at the very thought. But not anymore.

There was a time when the veteran quarterback coach believed that only bad things could happen when a quarterback scrambled all over the place. Treating NFL football like a game of Madden almost always led to fumbles, interceptions and injuries, almost always sabotaging victory.

But that was before Smith started coaching the Seattle Seahawks' Russell Wilson last season, before Wilson started making magic on seemingly every scramble.

Now?

"When that happens, I start getting happy," Smith says of Wilson's penchant for running around the backfield. "Something good's about to happen. That's what's happened in these two years. When Russell starts going, something good happens."

One of Smith's first decisions was to let Wilson play. Smith prepared to coach him by watching tapes of the youngster at Wisconsin, and he saw a quarterback who was "terrific outside the pocket," rolling out with poise, eyes always downfield.

Instead of forcing Wilson to stay in the pocket and work through his progressions, to learn to play like Peyton Manning, Smith encouraged the improv act. In practices, three or four plays a session, Wilson ditches the play and his receivers "react to it," Smith says.

"My personal impetus was 'Let's let him go,'" says Smith. "Just let him play and see what happens before we start changing him into something else. We pretty much let him go from Day 1, because when he gets out, he makes great decisions."

If Russell Wilson can make good decisions on Sunday night at MetLife Stadium, he may finally change the NFL's perception of the dual-threat quarterback. For the second straight year, the Super Bowl will pit new school against old school, as the super-shifty Wilson leads his upstart Seahawks against the Denver Broncos and Manning, the finest drop-back passer of this generation.

It's another chance to give credibility to the *Great Running Quarterback Revolution* that has seemed on the horizon for years. Throughout the annals of NFL history, a drop back quarterback has almost always hoisted the Lombardi Trophy. That's fueled the idea that a franchise needs a classic QB to win titles, forcing teams to ponder more versatile signal-callers with extra care.

But if Wilson can beat the legend of Manning in Super Bowl XLVIII, he could singlehandedly change that notion, forcing league insiders to view ultra-athletic QBs as more than a fad...

"The pocket passers, I feel like they have to give all that extra studying," says Jackson, (Wilson's backup in Seattle), who recalls how he himself relied on athleticism when he entered the NFL in 2006. "They can't move, so once things break down its pretty much over. Guys that are mobile, the play breaks down and they move, and it's a whole different play."

"In this day and age, the defensive linemen are so talented that you have to move most of the time," Wilson says. "Not all the time, but a lot of times, you have to move one (step), move two (steps). You have to have the ability to do that."

Multi-Threat Highlights & History

Russell Wilson

Youth

Russell Wilson started playing football as a four-year-old and honed his throwing skills by throwing the ball to his brother who was a fleet-footed receiver. Although he had considerable foot speed, it was Russell Wilson's strong arm that eventually helped him earn a starting job for the Collegiate School as a sophomore where he took his first steps towards becoming a huge star that he is today.

At school, Russell had an eye for football, basketball and baseball but it was football where he excelled more than anything. In his early years, Russell started at cornerback and according to many of his former coaches, was a very good lock-down corner, something not many people know. At a very young age, Russell Wilson was able to get the distance on his throws.

High School

Under the tutelage of coach Charlie McFall, Russell Wilson led Collegiate School to the 2004 state championship and also earned All-State honors. In the same year, he was named the Richmond Times Dispatch Player of the Year. In 2005, Wilson threw for 3,287 yards and 40 touchdowns and rushed for 634 yards and 15 touchdowns. In the same year, he was named an all-district, all-region and all-state player and was again named the Richmond Times-Dispatch Player of the Year.

He threw for 3,009 yards, 34 touchdowns and seven interceptions as a senior in 2006 while also rushing for 1,132 yards and 18 touchdowns. In the same year, he was named an all-conference and all-state player as well as conference player of the year. For his performance in the state championship win, he was featured in Sports Illustrated Magazine. Apart from playing football, Wilson was also a member of collegiate basketball and baseball teams.

College

In the spring of 2007, Wilson was selected in the 41st round by the Baltimore Orioles and although tempted to sign, he chose not to, deciding a college education was more important. Arriving in Raleigh as a redshirt, Russell Wilson sat out his first football season but did play for the Wolfpack baseball team as a freshman.

At the start of the 2008 season, Wilson had to compete with two other players for a starting spot but by midseason, he secured a permanent starting slot under coach Tom O'Brien. November was a perfect month for Wilson and the Wolfpack as they beat Duke, Wake Forest, UNC and Miami.

That month paved the way for NC State in the Papa John's Bowl against Rutgers. By halftime of that game, Russell guided his team to a 17-6 lead with 232 yards and then scored 13 points in the final period to guarantee his team a victory. He was named the ACC Rookie of the Year. As a freshman, Wilson threw for 17 touchdowns with a solitary interception. Moreover, he completed 150 of 275 passes for 1,995 yards and also ran four touchdowns. In the same year, he broke Andre Woodson's all-time NCAA record. In the 2009 campaign, Wilson threw for 3,027 yards with 31-TDs against 11-interceptions.

2010 was the most effective season for Wilson in which he led the ACC in passing yards and total offense. He completed 308 passes for 3,563 yards with only 14 interceptions. He was also the top rushing QB in the conference with 435 yards and nine touchdowns. In one of the most memorable games of that season, NC State defeated Florida State 28-24 at a time when the Seminoles were in the top 20. Trailing 24-21 in the final period, Russell Wilson brought his team back for the win.

In the last game of his junior year, Wilson guided his team to a 23-7 win over West Virginia in the Champs Sports Bowl as NC State sneaked into the top 25 year-end rankings. In 2011, Wilson could have entered the NFL draft but decided to transfer to the University of Wisconsin and play under the tutelage of Badgers' coach Bret Bielema who allowed him to play baseball that summer too. He played 61 games for the Class-A Asheville Tourists and batted .228 with three home runs.

Wilson arrived in Madison for the 2011 season to take over an already talented squad that went 11-2 the year before and played in the Rose Bowl. By then, Rick Tolzien, their previous star quarterback had graduated with the team desperate to recruit an experienced leader. And Russell destined to fill the role for one year.

It took him just three weeks to digest the entire playbook and he was subsequently named team captain. In his Badgers debut, Wilson dropped a whopping 51 points on UNLV with six of those coming from a 46-yard TD run. Wisconsin, courtesy of Russell's pinpoint passing, outscored their opponents by a jaw-dropping 301-58 margin.

The Badgers were first in the Big Ten's Leaders Division and earned the right to play in the first Big Ten Championship Game against Michigan State, in what turned out to be an entertaining and high scoring game. Russell made the play of the game on fourth down at the Michigan State 43-yard line, handing his team their historic win.

The QB twisted away from a near-sack and launched a desperate pass toward Jeff Duckworth who caught the ball deep in the red zone. Montee Ball ran for his fourth TD the next play, as the Badgers won 42-39 with Wilson was named MVP.

Russell Wilson's stock had risen in his final college season where he completed 72.8% of his passes and set an FBS record with a passing efficiency rating of 191.8. His 33 scoring tosses were a school record and the second all-time in Big Ten history. In December 2011, Wilson was named a third team All-American by Yahoo Sports and finished ninth in the voting for the Heisman Trophy with 52 points.

Pros

In 2012, Russell Wilson was picked up from the third-round of the NFL draft by the Seattle Seahawks and was not expected to be the starting quarterback in his first season. However, his performances in training camp impressed everyone and had a dream first season in which he threw for 3,113 yards, completed 64 percent of his passes, 26 touchdowns and only 10 interceptions.

In his first ever NFL game, Wilson threw 18 completions on 34 attempts for 153 yards, 1 touchdown and 1 interception. For his week 10 performance in the 28-7 win over the New York Jets, Wilson was named Pepsi NFL Rookie of Week. In that game, he threw 12 completions on 19 attempts for 188 yards and 2 touchdowns along with 7 rushing attempts for 34 yards.

Week 13 saw him named NFC Offensive Player of the Week and FedEx Air Player of the Week for his performance in the 23-17 Seahawks win over the Chicago Bears. He was then named NFL Offensive Rookie of the Month for December 2012 after his team went 5-0 with Wilson achieving a passer rating of 115.2. In the 2012 regular seasons, Wilson was ranked fourth in the NFL in passer rating as he beat the previous rookie record set by Ben Roethlisberger back in 2004.

He also tied Peyton Manning's record of most touchdowns thrown by a rookie by throwing 3,118 yards and 26 touchdowns. In his first season, Wilson helped his team to the playoffs and due to his performances, was selected as an alternate for the 2013 Pro Bowl.

At the Pro Bowl, he threw 8 completions on 10 attempts for 98 yards, 3 touchdowns and no interceptions while boasting a rating of 147.1.

His stats in his first NFL season were, 32 games, 6,475 yards passing, 52 passing TDs, 19 INTs, 63.6 percent pass completion, 100.6 QB rating, 1,028 yards rushing, 5 rushing TDs and 16 fumbles.

Russell Wilson and the Seahawks entered the 2013 campaign with a weight of expectations and after an opening week win over Cam Newton and the Carolina Panthers, Russell and co squared off with Colin Kaepernick and the 49ers who were the defending NFC champions. Playing at home, Russell Wilson guided his team to what was a sheer demolition of the reigning champs 29-3. In the first 11 games of the season, Wilson was among the Top 10 in completion percentage, touchdowns and QB rating.

In the game against Tampa Bay in early November, Russell Wilson was the architect of one of the greatest comebacks in team history. The Seahawks were trailing 21-0 in the dying embers of the first half but they managed to bridge the gap to 24-17 in the fourth quarter. With just two minutes left on the clock, Wilson lofted a 10-yard scoring pass to Doug Baldwin to tie the score. He then led a nine-play drive in OT to set up the winning field goal by Steven Hauschka.

In another nail-biting encounter, Wilson again proved his mettle for the team.

The Seahawks were down 20-6 against the Texans with only 8:24 left in the fourth quarter, they faced a fourth-and-three at the Houston Texans' seven-yard line. The Seahawks chose to go for it and ran a bootleg that called for their rookie quarterback to roll out to his right. As a counter measure, linebacker Whitney Mercilus was sent up the field off the edge to contain. By all rights, the play should have been a bust, as the Seahawks should have been forced to turn the ball over on downs as a consequence, allowing Houston to go on and register a win.

Wilson however, maneuvered Mercilus into slowing down for a second then ran right around him and gained enough yards for a first down. The touchdown was scored by running back Marshawn Lynch on the next play to put his team back in the game. Although this play goes into the stats sheet as a four yard run, it is perhaps the best example of how much of a nuisance Russell Wilson can be for his opponents, especially when it comes to crunch time.

Seattle went on to finish 13-3 in the regular season thanks to Russell Wilson's performances throughout the calendar year, and became the clear favorite to represent the NFC in Super Bowl XLVIII. Wilson ended the year with 26 touchdown passes with just seven interceptions. His QB rating was 101.2 as he became the first quarterback in the Super Bowl era to post a 100-plus passer rating in each of his first two seasons. In January 2014, Wilson helped the Seahawks beat the San Francisco 49ers in the NFC Championship game 23-17 as the Seattle made it to the Super Bowl.

The Seattle Seahawks steamrolled Denver Broncos in Super Bowl XLVIII and much of the credit for such the dominating display goes to their star quarterback Russell Wilson. In the Super Bowl XLVIII, Wilson threw for 206 yards, 2 touchdowns and no interceptions for a passer rating of 123.1 as Seattle dismantled Denver Broncos 43-8.

2

SCATBACK-QUARTERBACK

The NFL Hall of Fame celebrates the highlights and histories of one-dimensional quarterback heroes. But the times are a changing... One of the most exciting times in NFL football history is upon us, as a new paradigm quarterback is trending. And lo and behold, a journalist-prophet arises to articulate it for us all. Thank you Samuel.

Reviewing a few conclusions from the first chapter:

1) A new school v. old school struggle is happening in the NFL today as the position and traditional role of QB adapts to the quickest defenses in the history of the game.

2) A new QB model embracing improvisation and spontaneous read option plays is challenging the traditional QB model and playbook of the past.

3) NFL owners and coaches will embrace new improvisational offensive schemes to maximize the natural talents and developed skills of multi-threat playmaker QB's who will establish new standards for average "combined" rushing and passing yardage totals.

The multi-threat playmaker quarterback model is taking over, as traditional pocket passers enjoy their last hurrah, before they fade into the pages of history. Do you remember how soccer-style field goal kickers replaced old straight-leg field goal kickers? Or how goal posts were moved from the goal line to the back of the end zone? Same as making extra points after touchdowns…

A changing of the guard is occurring in the NFL right now. This coming season, and it will be coming again next year. You'll be watching it on TV, if you're not sitting comfortably in a modern-day Roman Coliseum watching the gladiators play live.

On your couch or in your armchair, from your seat in an NFL stadium… What people will continue to see unfolding is… A changing of the guard.

Russell Wilson proved it. Winning the Super Bowl with Seattle's super-quick defensive play, and his overall good quarterback play plus the critical gains he had on several key scramble rushes.

Colin Kaepernick could have been the first example of this new model winning a Super Bowl, if San Francisco's defense hadn't given up 34-points. Spectacular in the regular season and throughout the playoffs, Kaepernick proved having a multi-threat player at the helm makes sense. Blowing naysayers out of the way he rushed for 181-yards in one game. Yep, you heard me right. It's incredible to imagine! Almost unthinkable that a quarterback would pick up close to 200-yards on the ground… But he did, and if one quarterback can do it once then another one could do it again.

Of course another multi-threat playmaker quarterback could do it again. Why not? It's rather easy when you're quick enough and fast enough, and hard to tackle. What makes me say it's easy for great runners is how defensive players have to respect your passing. What makes it harder for the defenders is how multi-threat runner passers can escape when one-dimensional quarterbacks would get sacked for a loss, or have to throw the ball away to avoid a sack.

This is an important advantage for an offense, because the tin soldier quarterback gives up negative sack yardage or penalty yardage from intentional grounding far too often. Where, it's no big deal for a multi-threat quarterback to extend a play with his feet. I did it myself.

You buy a second or two, or as long as possible. This gives the receivers time to get open downfield, or time for the field to open up for an easy 4- or 5-yard gain on the ground. If you're fast, speed dominates. When nobody's faster and you break into the clear you're going to pick up big yardage. Since speed does dominate… If you get 1-step on the field you are going to score. I did it all the time. Once I had a step on the rest of the field, nobody caught me from behind. When I was in a full, unimpeded sprint to the goal line I scored.

Quarterbacks who can run for it, or pull up and throw are the hardest guys for defenders to stop. The future of football will be founded on multi-talented quarterbacks like this. Eventually, the traditional pocket passer of NFL lore will be no more, except in the NFL Football Hall of Fame. Where their place in football history will remain secure.

No insult intended to those quarterbacks. They will live on as heroes in the hearts and minds of faithful fans. But the new model replacing them cannot be stopped from taking over. It's already too late, sorry. Coming in a bungling way, with the Wildcat offense establishing the logic of a short-direct-snap to a runner threat so 11-guys are involved in the offensive play instead of only 10… like the drop back passer model. With a quarterback who mostly fakes like he's playing when he's not passing or after he hands off.

Too often old-style quarterbacks took the snap, handed it or pitched it to someone else, then were out of the play. So only 10-offensive players were running the rest of the play against 11-defenders… How dumb. Why design an offensive strategy around a leader-player who is routinely completely out of the play, acting like he's still in the play?

But the Wildcat was too predictable. The snap would always go to the designated Wildcat runner. Typically the team's best running back and a pure runner who never passed the ball, and the defenders knew a run was coming.

Thank you Russell Wilson, and Seattle. Thank you Colin Kaepernick, and San Francisco. When more team owners awaken to the reality of what these two teams have made very obvious. Fans from all NFL teams will be closer to seeing the new and improved offenses of the future competing against each other every game.

A far more spontaneous and fun style of football is knocking at the door. Warming up the remote you're holding in your hand. The multi-threat quarterback of the future will be proficient at running and improvising. In the future, the quarterback model will feature playmakers that excel at making plays with both rushing and passing skills. If it doesn't work perfectly, it works imperfectly. Either way it works.

That's how I played as a kid and it was a blast. I improvised, beating opponents imperfectly. I knew I could break any play. I knew I had the speed. I did it all the time. I don't deserve all the credit, my teammates paved the way, but they knew they could count on me too. I was born fast. I could break any play and often did. Turning broken plays into long rushing touchdowns was my thing. Not a bad fallback option for a play that didn't work to begin with.

Score a touchdown instead!

I was most dangerous when forced to improvise as a running quarterback. Batten down the hatches. Hold on, and watch out… I was thinking "touchdown" every play. And I made it to the end zone eluding tacklers and breaking tackles all the time. Making moves that left defenders breathing violence at me – and all the girls holding their breaths.

I'd make a great spokesman for this kind of play. And here's what I'd say:

Somebody needs to get serious and wake up! Accept it. This "reality" is here to stay. Stop fighting it with deficient mindsets. Get with the program. Figure it out, please. Somebody. Move forward for a change. Believe in what's coming enough to plan ahead for it and go after the athletes who will be taking the game there. Target the best of the best multi-threat players coming out of college.

Yes, stop fidgeting like this makes you feel uncomfortable, and figure out how to find the greatest multi-threat playmakers in each draft. Simple enough, isn't it? Logical. Practical. Figure out a way to test the athletes for their multi-threat skills and instincts. **So you can identify them!** Then set up your program to develop these playmakers and maximize the intangible advantages they bring to a team.

A form of testing that defines new standards of evaluation needs to be developed, to specifically evaluate the potential of multi-threat quarterback talents. And here's what I would recommend, thinking about how to do it…

1. Evaluate the multi-talented prospect's <u>quickness</u>, <u>speed</u> and <u>agility</u> for a ratio of "elusiveness." How hard they are to catch and stop. Create some ratio that identifies the athlete by testing for these specific physical abilities.

2. Evaluate the multi-talented prospect's "drive" component. Create a way to evaluate, analyze and compare the athlete's <u>drive</u>, <u>volition</u> and <u>will-to-win</u>. Combine these testing results in some form of ID so you can compare athletes by this means.

There you have it: The magic math of the future!

Identify the players with the most natural scatback skills, who can pass the ball and have a strong will to win. So these athletes can be developed into the multi-threat running quarterback playmakers of the future.

Scat·back

Pronunciation: skat-bak

Noun / 1945

: An <u>offensive</u> back in football who is an especially fast and elusive ball carrier, skilled at escaping tacklers.

That was me except I could pass too. That was my game as a kid. I was a born winner at heart who led my young teams by example, giving everything I had every play. And I had a lot to give. Not the strongest arm, but my instincts and reaction time made up for it and my running threat opened receiver routes.

We hardly ever had sack-yardage work against us. If I didn't get back to the line of scrimmage like Dad drilled into my head, then I picked up yardage.

Dad said, "If it goes wrong and the play breaks down, get back to the line of scrimmage. Don't get sacked." I did what he told me and fought back when sacks seemed imminent. I could not get sacked, was my attitude. That's what my dad told me and it's a different game when a quarterback rarely gets sacked.

Today's gridiron stars are the most gifted to ever play the game. As a combined force, the players of today are taking the game of football to exciting new levels of athletic prowess. Unshackled by new offensive schemes and playbooks, these guys will be setting new records that make the game of the past look old.

Watching Colin Kaepernick in his great come-from-behind Super Bowl showed where things are trending. His powerful second half performance fell just short, but seeing that game took me back to what happened in my first year of football.

I was in the 4th grade when we made it to the championship game with a fun group of kids. And my blockers only had one year of experience, so I got rushed a lot and had to run around to make plays work sometimes. Fortunately for us, I could escape tacklers and make something out of nothing.

By the end of that first season we were playing great and peaking at the right time and the championship game was our closest game all season. But we didn't quite get it done like I expected. We didn't quite win. We lost. Had our chances, but we were first-year players so... Live and learn. But I know how Kaepernick felt losing a championship he could have won.

If you never did it yourself it's outrageously fun playing football like Russell Wilson and Colin Kaepernick. Where you're free to run. When NFL offensive playbooks catch up to the multi-threat playmakers who can run and pass, fans will see more spectacular performances like Kaepernick's 181-yard record day.

Kaepernick's game-of-a-lifetime stats are one of the most impressive statements to the potential of developing the multi-threat quarterback model.

The best part of having players like him is how the honesty of their enthusiasm can infect their teams. Suddenly, all the players feel as invincible as the gifted star playmaker. They "want to" feel that way, and have their own star potential inside. Give them a reason to believe and they will. It's fun to see how an entire team can get infused with a will to do great things and be great playmakers who make great plays and have great days like Kaepernick's day against Green Bay.

I think a healthy Kaepernick could become a Super Bowl Champion if San Francisco's defense improves, and assuming he doesn't get on the cover of a Madden Football video game any time soon.

Multi-Threat Highlights & History

Colin Kaepernick

Youth

Born on November 3, 1987 in Milwaukee, Wisconsin, Colin Rand Kaepernick was adopted by Teresa and Rick Kaepernick when he was five weeks old. As a baby, his health was far from perfect as he suffered from chronic ear infection, which was cured later on. In the early 1990s, when he moved with his family to the West Coast Kaepernick began competing in youth sports leagues. He took to football right away and made it look easy due to his strength, quickness and coordination, beyond his age.

As a youngster, he took the responsibility for his team's kicking assignments and was usually found on the defensive line. However, at the age of nine, he started playing quarterback. Football however, was just one of several sports he played. When not on the gridiron, Kaepernick was pitching in Little League or playing basketball.

While at Dutcher Elementary School, Colin's teacher gave him an assignment to write a letter to his future self. In his letter, Kaepernick wrote he hoped to go to a good college and get drafted by the San Francisco 49ers or Green Bay Packers since he wanted to one day replace Brett Favre for the Cheese heads.

High School

In 2002, Kaepernick enrolled in Pitman High School and entered their football program as a promising athlete who could throw the ball to home plate at over 70mph and also throw tight spirals for up to 50 yards.

At Pitman, the future NFL star earned all-state recognition in all three of his favorite sports and led the Pride football squad to their first-ever state playoff triumph. His performances also alerted college football scouts who had to compete with baseball recruiters. While making his mark in football,

Colin's baseball skills were equally jaw dropping with the youngster already having tossed a pair of no-hitters and gotten his fast ball into the low 90's. He was offered a baseball scholarships from Tennessee, Arizona State and Notre Dame.

But Kaepernick's heart was in football, and his coach Larry Nigro compiled a video of Kaepernick's performances and sent it to more than 100-schools after his junior season. Hoping to get more visibility, he enrolled in several college football camps and impressed University of Nevada-Reno's coaches with his foot speed and strong arm.

When Kaepernick decided baseball would not in the picture, he was offered a scholarship by head coach Chris Ault. One reason Ault was so desperate to acquire the young Kaepernick was how impressed one of his assistants was by the player's performance in a basketball game where he entered the floor with high fever and singlehandedly won the game for his team.

College

In 2006, Kaepernick red-shirted and added more muscle to his lanky frame. In the fifth game of the 2007 campaign, starting QB Nick Graziano was injured in the first half of game five and he was brought on the field as the signal-caller. What happened next is now part of Wolf pack folklore.

Kaepernick helped his team torch Fresno State with 384-yards and four touchdowns, and in his first start against Boise State (nationally ranked) he again showed how good he was at QB. The remainder of the season Graziano was on the bench as Kaepernick finished with 19-touchdowns and only three interceptions. He was the fourth best QB in the nation, boasting a 161.06 QB rating.

Kaepernick became only the fifth player in NCAA history to amass 2,000 passing yards and 1,000 rushing yards in a single season, in the 2008 campaign. In that groundbreaking season, he passed for 2,849 yards and ran for 1,130. Accounting for 39 touchdowns, of which 22 were through the air and 17 on the ground. At the end of the season, Kaepernick became only the second sophomore after Marshall Faulk (who achieved the feat in 1992) in WAC history to be named Offensive Player of the Year.

In 2009, Colin Kaepernick guided Nevada to a second-place finish in the Western Athletic Conference and for his efforts, was named team MVP for the second time. In that season, he threw for 2,052-yards and ran for 1,183, becoming the first player in the history of NCAA to have back-to-back 2,000-1,000 yard campaigns. He was also part of the first ever college team to have three 1,000-yard rushers in the same backfield. This led Nevada to being in the College Football Hall of Fame.

In his senior year, Kaepernick won the WAC title and what was even more important was that he was the architect of his team's overtime win against Boise State. Nevada won the game 34-31 in Kaepernick's final home game and his performance is still considered as the highpoint in the history of his school's football program. He became the only passer to throw and run for 20-touchdowns in a single season along with Tim Tebow and Cam Newton.

Pros

For the 2011 NFL draft, analysts predicted Kaepernick would go late in the first round or early second. When he was still on the board after the second round, the San Francisco 49ers traded up and grabbed him with a pick that belonged to the Denver Broncos in a deal that cost the 49ers three lower draft picks.

He joined the franchise as back-up to Alex Smith. In his first season, Kaepernick watched Smith rally the 49ers to the NFC title game. In his first season, he saw less game-time but showed enough that his NFL future looked bright.

Then Jim Harbaugh decided to use Kaepernick in the Wildcat formation during 2012. The rookie took to the plan easily and his strong arm and speed of a sprinter created havoc for enemy defenses. Things were going more or less according to plan until Week 10 when Smith left the game against St. Louis Rams with a concussion.

Kaepernick came in and did more than just well, and in the following week earned the starting spot against the Bears. Many 49ers fans had doubts about the youngster against the Chicago defense. However, Kaepernick enjoyed a great game, completing 16 of his 23 pass attempts for 246 yards and two touchdowns.

With Week 12 approaching and Smith recovered, coach Harbaugh had a dilemma but chose to rest the experienced QB in favor of Kaepernick. And the youngster did not disappoint. He did extremely well, creating enough time to throw to his receivers and making several good runs, and passing for one touchdown in an impressive 31-21 win for the 49ers against the New Orleans Saints.

After seeing such strong displays, Harbaugh stuck with Kaepernick as his starter. In the final five weeks of the season, the 49ers won every game and won the NFC West Championship. In his first full season with the NFL franchise, Kaepernick registered 1,814 passing yards with 10 touchdowns and just three interceptions. He also ran for 415 yards and five touchdowns (averaging 6.6 yards per carry) to cap off a remarkable season.

 In the first playoff game against the Packers, Kaepernick threw for 256 yards and two touchdowns in a 45-31 win. Once again, it was his powerful legs that made the difference. On designed plays, he ran over 100 yards, and on wild scrambles registered another 75 yards. He finished the game with 181 yards on the ground breaking the rushing yards record set by Michael Vick in 2002. Green Bay had no idea what hit them as the 49ers moved on to the NFC Championship against the Atlanta Falcons at the Georgia Dome.

The Falcons seemed to have things working well, but Kaepernick brought his team back. Leading the 49ers on an 80-yard drive, highlighted by a long completion to Vernon Davis, and capped off by a 15-yard scoring run by LaMichael James. With less than a minute left to half time, Tony Gonzalez's touchdown for Atlanta brought things close as the two sides went inside the dressing room.

In the second half, rallied by Kaepernick, the 49ers defense neutralized the threat posed by Matt Ryan, and Kaepernick completed several clutch throws, finishing the game with 233 yards on 16-for-21 passing.

Super Bowl XLVII was history in the making before the ball was kicked as Jim and John Harbaugh squared off in the first coaching matchup of brothers. However, the focus was on Kaepernick. It appeared Baltimore would run away with the game but a power outage changed the game. When the lights came back on, Kaepernick came on with them, and helped his team steamroll over the Ravens.

The star led his team to a pair of touchdowns in the 3rd quarter and in the final period was involved in another scoring drive with a 15-yard score. He compiled almost 400 yards and scored two touchdowns. In the 2013 season, Kaepernick threw for 21 touchdowns with only eight interceptions, 3,197 yards and boasted a QB passer rating of 91.6. In his 92 rushes, he finished with 524 rushing yards and four rushing TDs, averaging 5.7-yards per carry.

On June 4, 2014, Kaepernick signed a six-year contract extension with the 49ers worth $126 million, including $61-million guaranteed.

There are few quarterbacks in the NFL who can make defenses look bad the way Kaepernick does. His success in the 2012 season was attributed to him being an unknown and though opponents did prepare themselves the next season, they also learned the QB's talents were diverse. With great arm strength and accuracy to drill precise passes, Kaepernick was a nightmare for every opposing team. His ability to scramble out of tight spots and rack up big yards makes him a special multi-threat NFL talent.

3

KID'S PLAY

Lest we forget... Let us remember. Football is a kid's game first.

When I was a kid there was a lot of expectation I'd be a chip off the old block like my father. It was a foregone conclusion around my house that I would follow in my father's footsteps and play in the NFL. Like sons of other old-time football families I was born with the talent to deliver. Then I started playing and left everybody's jaws hanging open.

Whatever dad had, I had a double portion. Though I lost a championship my first year, the next year I came back determined. I would not let it slip away a second time. When I went to my dad and asked to call my own plays... NO was the answer. Then he told me the news I mentioned in the Intro, where the league agreed to ban quarterbacks from running after taking the snap.

Not okay! Not fair.

Based on that rule created to stop ME, I no longer had the option to run-or-pass. I could pass or hand off, or pitch. But I could NOT run if I took the snap. There was no way to grind my teeth harder than when I got that news. But the league agreed with the other coaches and made the new rule to stop me. So there was nothing I could do about it.

Then dad reworked our playbook around a new backfield with not one, but two quarterbacks. So I could take a pitch from our other quarterback, who took the original hike from center. And I would still be free to run or pass like before the rule. Dual quarterbacks! Not only were the other coaches unable to stop me, but our new scheme had a new twist that made us more unpredictable than I was by myself, and more difficult to defend.

It was fun playing with two quarterbacks like that. I loved it. We created on the fly and made the most of it. Winning back-to-back championships while everybody tried to figure us out. It needed no justification or explanation. It worked. All you had to do was watch us, or play against us if you wanted to see for yourself. My compatriot QB was not the runner I was, but played the position well otherwise. With two passers we were totally unpredictable.

Imagine what it felt like losing the championship my first year in football. Then coming back to win back-to-back championships in 5th and 6th grades. That was the greatest feeling of my life at the time. Back-to-back Champions!

Had the league not made the rule to stop me, it would never have happened. That's how I came to realize what a great idea it is to have two quarterbacks in the game at the same time. How unfortunate for the defense! Our new look offense had so many options coming and going, there was no way to anticipate what we might do next. One play we would look traditional. The next, do something never seen before. The play after that... who had any idea? Certainly NOT the defenses we demolished two-years in a row!

Undefeated at midseason in the 5th grade I started pressing dad to let me call the plays. We were winning he said, "If it ain't broke don't fix it." But I challenged him, saying I had earned it. We were winning because of me, not his play calling. I made every play work. I was delivering on the field.

When dad called the plays, he sent players in with one index card showing the play. The card had the play on each side showing the play going left, or going right. When I started calling plays we had to devise a way I could hold all the cards so they wouldn't go flying when I got tackled. Simplest solution? A flip up hole-punch card system with some string and a custom pocket sewed into my football pants by my mom. Where I could stuff the cards between each play.

I finally got dad to agree to let me call the plays the 1st-quarter. And he would take over at halftime if I was struggling. That was the last time he called the plays for me, because at halftime of the next game we were crushing the other team and I was calling a good game.

After losing the first year, I had to wait for my next chance to win my first championship. Against the team with the meanest looking coach in the league... Man, I was pumped.

They were bigger than we were with one guy a foot taller than our pint-sized E-brother defensive backs. Two little guys who had a double-forceful will to win like me. I bet on those guys like they bet on me. The game was close from beginning to end, but we never trailed. It was more dominant than it seemed actually, and they fought hard. But how fun it was to redeem myself and win that championship game.

It's hard to say what it felt like... holding that little trophy up like a real champion.

The little gold playmaker on top of my trophy. With his arm stretched out to stop an invisible tackler, his leg rising to simulate running. Connected to the base only by one golden shoe. In my mind, I was the guy on top of that trophy. It was cool putting him on my shelves in my bedroom where everybody could see him. Friends, cousins, sister's friends, my parents.

By 6th grade we were the team to beat. The team with the dual quarterbacks like nobody else played. Sounded crazy, but it worked. Opposing defenses never had the same certainty of what was coming next. Most often I took a pitch from the quarterback and we ran our plays so I was free to run or pass.

Facing our arch-nemesis for the tiebreaker championship was our biggest challenge of the three-seasons our team played together. Though we scored twice, we gave up two scores so we were tied 13-13 at the half. Struggling through the 3rd quarter we finally broke the deadlock and scored on a 60-yard pass and run that looked like a pitch sweep. We had been running the same pitch sweep both directions, when I suddenly rose up and spiraled a lofted pass downfield to one of my receivers.

Catching it in stride he turned up field and ran for the long tie-breaking score. That gave us a 7-point lead and momentum. We scored one more time from 50-yards out on a wild scramble-run that had me dancing down the sideline to stay in bounds to make it 27-13 by the end of the game.

How could I not love that style of play? The running passer playmaker I played myself. Even if my football days were cut short, I got to live that experience before the injuries.

Back in the day I remember watching Roger Staubach and Fran Tarkenton battle it out on one of only "three" total TV channels. Two early multi-threat quarterbacks who could make plays with their passing and scrambling. Neither had much speed but both would run to pick up first downs to keep drives alive. Like John Elway scrambled for key yards when he and Terrell Davis were leading Denver to back-to-back championships.

I played like that when I was a kid when my team won back-to-back championships. Running our one-of-a-kind dual quarterback backfield while everybody else tried to slow it down. Good luck with that.

Years later I had the privilege to do it all over again, and more, when I got to coach my son's football team and decided to reinvent the old "future of football" more-than-one-quarterback offense. As head coach there was nothing to stop me. I could do whatever I wanted. So our team had no "pocket passer" and no pocket passing plays. The key to our success: A revolutionary playbook.

How liberating!

After evaluating my team I picked the top three multi-talents as my "multi-threat" QB-Unit of the future. Not one, not two, but three multi-threat playmakers to replace the one-dimensional pocket passer concept.

The three most natural athletes who could pass, catch and run. And I worked to help them improve their passing, running and catching skills. Being natural athletes it all came quickly to them as they developed into our Multi-Threat QB Unit.

We had read option plays for our best three playmakers where they could share taking snaps, share passing, share running and share catching. There were no rules prohibiting us from playing like that, so we gave youth football a whole new look with our "Unit of Three" co-leader starters. Instead of the single one-dimensional individual quarterback who is not a running threat.

How did it look? We never took a snap from under center. We never started a single play going backwards first. Like quarterbacks take a snap at the line and retreat backwards in the NFL. We eliminated taking the snap directly from under center. Strategically, going the wrong direction first makes no sense.

We had a short direct snap that went to one of two multi-threat playmakers. Lining up two quarterbacks behind center. The snapped ball had to go a little right, or a little left of directly behind the center. Imagine a V, with the bottom of the V being the center. My two backs would line up at the top of the V. So they were split apart a few yards. The center would snap the ball to one of them. We did this to create doubt so the defenders would not automatically know who was getting the snap.

When a snap goes to a traditional pocket passing quarterback, the defense knows "exactly" where he's going to set up and throw. No mystery to it. It's a given. They know already. Defenses know in advance the precise location a traditional pocket passer retreats to try and pass from, on almost every pass he throws.

That's a nice advantage. To know exactly who is getting the ball every snap, then know exactly where they're going with the ball after the snap on most pass plays. It makes no sense to be that predictable. No military could survive by such a misguided notion of strategy. That never happened in our offense!

The snap was not going directly back to a single player everybody knew was getting it, but left-or-right behind center, to one of two different playmakers.

And nobody had any idea if they were going to run or pass or pitch or hand off, or what they might do. Nobody knew who was getting the ball every snap. Nobody knew where the player getting the ball might go to set up to pass. Or, if he might roll out and throw or run or maybe pitch the ball.

That uncertainty played in our favor. We ran a high percentage of the time because our plays were run/pass options with the instruction to run first if there were 4-yards to gain without risking a bad throw or dropped pass. We had a mix of pure running plays, run-first pass option plays and pure pass plays for longer yardage. But most of our plays were read option run-or-pass plays. We also shifted our line at times so the center was not in the middle.

How did it work? Great. We won one championship, and lost one championship. My son's team finished first, then second in consecutive years. Pretty good for an unconventional style of play to deliver those results! I only coached two years, but along with my personal experience from playing as a kid, I got the privilege of testing the theory, that two QB's are better than one. And proved it is viable with quarterbacks who are scatback-like runners.

Our multi-threat playmakers didn't have the best individual stats. But collectively their combined passing, rushing and receiving yards had to be double that of any quarterback we faced.

What did it look like? More playmakers touched the ball every game all game long. What was one of the most distinct differences, compared to normal football. We never once had our starting quarterback knocked out of a game. How can you knock three guys out at once?

Here are the instructions I gave our QB Unit of three:

"If the center snaps it over your head and you don't catch it. That's your fault. He has someone about to smash into him. You're just standing there, watching and waiting. If he rolls the ball on the ground and it bounces away, and you don't catch it. That's your fault too. No matter what he does, it's your fault if you don't catch it.

"If you miss it, go get it as fast as you can. But before that, don't miss it. Unless you want to trade places with the center." Those were my instructions. And I told our center to make sure he got a good snap back.

So it was that, "The Three" never fumbled away a snap all season. Not that it went perfect every time, but they got the snap somehow or another. Which I told them was mainly due to our excellent center, Steven. The best center in the league, in my opinion.

Steven, who's father showed up to the first practice late, with Steven in tow. Then interrupted me while I was talking to our team. Saying he was sorry they were late but Steven wasn't really an athlete anyway. And he knew Steven couldn't really play football and would never score a touchdown because he was just an average kid. To which I nodded and motioned for him to leave please.

The huddle was hushed after that exchange.

I waited to speak then said, "Steven, come here." The players moved apart and made room for Steven to walk through to me. When his father was far enough away I asked, "Okay. How many of you think Steven is just average and can't play football, raise your hand?"

Nobody moved and no hands went up. Then I spoke to the boy directly saying, "Steven, I think you could be one of the most important players on this team! Do you believe me?" He looked up with a questioning squint and didn't answer.

"And I think you're gonna' score a touchdown," I said. Then I addressed the team and asked, "Who thinks Steven will score a touchdown this season? Raise your hand?" To which all hands shot up and everybody started moving again. It was a crucial moment in creating the right kind of sub-culture for the culture of our team. The culture within a culture at a core place in everybody's heart and soul that makes great teams great… What they all believe in, about each other and themselves.

The day Steven scored his touchdown I called timeout to have him come to the sideline first, then told him "Switch with X-Ray for the next play and tell him to snap the ball to you. When he snaps it you catch it no matter where it goes... Then score a touchdown. Okay?"

Steven smiled, said yes sir... ran to the huddle, called the play, got the snap and scored from 2-yards out for the final touchdown of the game. While back in the stands, Steven's dad was just beaming.

Highlights & History

Roger Staubach & Fran Tarkenton

Youth thru College

Fran Tarkenton moved to Georgia with his family at the age of 11. He had a distinguished high school career in Athens, earning all-state honors in football, basketball and baseball. He led the Athens High School Trojans to a state championship in 1955.

He enrolled at the University of Georgia in 1957 and as a freshman led Georgia's freshman team to an undefeated season. He was also an All-SEC sophomore team selection in 1958. One year later, the young quarterback would go on to lead the University of Georgia Bulldogs to the Southeastern Conference (SEC) title in 1959.

The Bulldogs' strong offensive unit that year drew nicknames like the "Tarkenton Raiders" and "Tarkenton's Music Makers". He led the SEC in passing completions and in the same year, set a conference record for completion percentage. On New Year's Day in 1960, Tarkenton led the Bulldogs to an Orange Bowl victory over Missouri.

In his senior season, Tarkenton was named the captain of his team and once again led the conference in total offense and passing yards and was named an All-American. As a reflection of his strong performance in the classroom he was selected as an Academic All-American.

Born on February 5, 1942 in Cincinnati, Ohio, Roger Staubach attended St. John the Evangelist Catholic School. It was at the New Mexico Military Institute in Roswell, New Mexico where Staubach got his first action of real football as a member of the NMMI Broncos football program.

He enlisted in the Navy where he became a quarterback for the Navy Midshipmen. It was there as a third-class midshipman (sophomore),

Staubach got his opportunity to play in the third game of the season against the University of Minnesota in 1962. In his second game, Staubach was the spark in his team's offense and went on to lead Navy to six TDs, threw for 99-yards and two TDs while running for 88-yards and another score as his team romped to a 41-0 win.

In the fabled Army-Navy game in front of President John Kennedy, Staubach guided his team to a memorable 34-14 win, throwing for two TDs and running for another. The next season was even better for the budding quarterback. As a junior, Staubach won the Heisman Trophy, Maxwell Award, and the Walter Camp Memorial Trophy as the Midshipmen registered a record 9-1 season with a final ranking of #2 in the nation.

In his three years at Navy, Staubach completed 292 of his 463 passes with 18-TDs, 19 interceptions and gained a school record of 4,253 yards of total offense. Till this day, Staubach is the last player from a military institution to win the Heisman Trophy. In a graduation ceremony after his senior season, The Naval Academy retired Staubach's jersey number (#12).

Pro

Fran Tarkenton was drafted by the Minnesota Vikings in third round of the 1961 NFL draft and was picked in the fifth round of the 1961 AFL draft by the Boston Patriots. At the age of 21, he signed with the Vikings and made his NFL debut against the Chicago Bears.

In that game, he came off the bench and helped his team to a comeback win by passing for 250 yards and four TD passes and ran for another. He is also the only player in the history of NFL to pass for four touchdowns on his NFL debut.

Tarkenton played for Vikings from 1961 to 1966 where he first instilled the idea of a mobile quarterback. Due to his innovation, he was given nicknames such as "The Mad Scrambler", "Frantic Fran" and "Scramblin' Fran". He was one of the first quarterbacks to frequently run around in the backfield to avoid being sacked and buy time to throw, or scramble up the field for gains on the ground.

In 1967, he was traded to the New York Giants and spent five seasons there. His arrival saw the Giants become from a basement team to a competitive one. In the 1972 season, Tarkenton was traded back to Minnesota and led the Vikings to three Super Bowls. After his performances in the 1975 season, Tarkenton won the NFL's MVP award and earned All-Pro honors. He was also second Team All-Pro in 1973 and earned All-NFC selections in 1972 and 1976. In total, Tarkenton played in nine Pro Bowls.

In what is still considered one of the most productive NFL careers, Tarkenton's 18 seasons in the NFL saw him complete 3,686 of 6,467 passes for 47,003 yards and 342 touchdowns with 266 interceptions. His career passing yards rank him 6th all-time while his 342 passing TD's place him 4th all-time in NFL history.

His impressive scrambling ability saw him rack up 3,674 rushing yards and 32 touchdowns for 675 carries. In 15 different seasons, Tarkenton ran for a touchdown, which is an NFL record. Along with Tobin Rote, he is the only NFL QB to rush for at least 300 yards in seven different seasons. Upon his retirement, Tarkenton held NFL records in pass attempts, yardage, completions and touchdowns; rushing yards by a quarterback and wins by a starting quarterback.

Minnesota Vikings #10 jersey was retired in Tarkenton's honor. He was given the Minnesota Vikings Ring of Honor and also named in their 25th and 40th anniversary team. He is also in the list of 50 Greatest Vikings players and in 1986, was inducted in the Pro Football Hall of Fame. In 1987, he was inducted in the College Football Hall of Fame.

Roger Staubach was a 10th-round future draft pick by the Dallas Cowboys in the 1964 NFL Draft. Due to his military commitment, the National Football League allowed the Cowboys to draft him a year before his college eligibility was over. Staubach joined the Dallas Cowboys as a 27-year-old rookie five years later in 1969 and became a starter in 1971.

Craig Morton began the season as a starter but following a defeat at the hands of the New Orleans Saints, Staubach was given the starting role. After a lot of rotation in quarterback role by coach Tom Landry, Staubach was given a starting role permanently in week eight where the team beat St. Louis Cardinals.

That win set a run of 10 consecutive victories for the Cowboys including the franchise's first ever Super Bowl win at the expense of the Miami Dolphins. In the Super Bowl VI on January 16, 1972, Staubach was named MVP after completing 12 out of 19 passes for 119 yards and two TDs and rushing for 18 yards.

Staubach missed most of the 1972 season with a dislocated shoulder but returned in style against the San Francisco 49ers in a division playoff game where he threw two touchdown passes in the dying ambers of the game to guide his team to a 30-28 win.

In 1977, Staubach led his team to a second Super Bowl where he threw for 183 yards and a touchdown with no interceptions as Dallas beat Denver Broncos 27-10. In his final NFL season in 1979, Staubach set career highs in pass completions, passing yards and touchdown passes with just eleven interceptions as the curtains closed on one of the most fabled careers in the history of NFL.

In his 11 NFL seasons, Staubach had 1,685 completions for 22,700 yards and 153 touchdowns with 109 interceptions. He also gained 2,264 rushing yards and scored 21 touchdowns on 410 carries. In four seasons (1971, 1973, 1978 and 1979), Staubach registered the highest passer rating in the NFL. In 1973, he led the league with 23 TD passes. He was named in the NFL 1970s All-Decade Team, Dallas Cowboys Ring of Honor and was an inductee in the 1985 Pro Football Hall of Fame. He has also been rated #46 NFL Player of All-time by nfl.com.

Comparing the two scrambling quarterbacks

Staubach never led the NFL in passing yards or passing touchdowns in the 1970s. Those accomplishments went to Fran Tarkenton. However, it was as a running quarterback where Roger Staubach surpassed Tarkenton. Staubach was an excellent playmaker of his era and rushed for 2,204 yards and 19 TDs, which is more than double the yards that Tarkenton amassed with his feet.

Tarkenton was a great leader who helped make the Vikings an exciting team in their early years. His ability to escape pressure and buy time to throw and give his receivers time to break containment and get open.

Despite his small frame, Tarkenton was an indestructible force. By buying extraordinary amount of time, Tarkenton didn't have to zip the ball to his receiver. Tarkenton's NFL legacy is not of a quarterback who did not win a Super Bowl.

In fact, it was a legacy of innovation and creativity. His style was a new philosophy in the NFL. What he started is still the norm today and is likely to continue to be thus for a long time. Today, most quarterbacks might not be able to run like Tarkenton, but they need to buy time with their feet in order to give sufficient time to their receivers to make a play.

Although he came in NFL very late as compared to most, Staubach's arrival was what Dallas Cowboys needed. Although they had decent quarterbacks in Craig Morton and Don Meredith, both had their own limitations. So the arrival of Staubach was a blessing for coach Tom Landry who liked the 27-year-old rookie from his first training session. All qualities that Landry expected from his players were to be found in the ex-Navy man. He had a strong and accurate arm, a quick release, saw the pass rush well and could get out of tight corners and avoid making mistakes.

Due to his agility, Staubach overcame errors and mistakes while getting his team downfield to make a big play, which most often resulted in victory. Staubach's ability to run with the ball literally changed the way the game was scouted and executed. While Tarkenton is considered the forerunner of the quarterbacks, it was Staubach who further exploited that style of playing, scrambling to get out of trouble, buy time and make plays on the run.

He used to run with the ball as a last result. Due to his innovative style, which usually always yielded positive outcomes, the idea of having a mobile quarterback gained universal acceptance. No longer would a team look for a "pocket passer" at quarterback although Dan Marino and Peyton have been notable exceptions.

The great quarterbacks since the Staubach era have had some degree of mobility, or stretching out a play. As important as his arm strength, quick release and ability to read defenses, Staubach's leadership qualities were equally important.

Tarkenton, despite his versatility as a runner and passer, he was the NFL All-Time leader in passing yards with 47,003 while Staubach's playmaking made him an innovator like no other.

4

GRIT & GRIND

As multi-threat quarterbacks have entered the NFL in recent years, some have been knocked out of the active rotation by injuries. Not surprisingly, those sliding to a stop on scrambles and runs faring better than those putting their bodies at risk taking direct hits from tacklers.

The greatest multi-threat playmakers are no more invincible from injury than anybody else. Ask Michael Vick, who has played outstanding when healthy and less outstanding when dealing with injuries. If a coach allows a player to keep playing when injured, he does the player a great disservice that will inevitably lead to a decline in performance.

The way the mind and body favor an injury is unstoppable. You can't keep your mind from instinctively sending your body messages – to take protective measures. It's written into your DNA. The subconscious takes over and you favor injuries in small, often undetectable ways. It's involuntary. I became living proof of this reality when I played hurt and kept getting hurt in my last year of football.

The natural subconscious favoring of an injury makes things slightly abnormal in an athlete's body. Instead of moving like he would if he was healthy, the player moves differently to slightly favor the injury, without even knowing he's doing it. Extended playing like this increases the odds an injured athlete will incur other injuries. You can get away with it for a while, but not forever.

In my early football campaigns it didn't matter how wild I played. I never suffered a single serious injury and had an absolute blast making plays as a multi-threat playmaker. Setting the stands a roar with my athletic, exciting, daring style of play. Like interception returns, or breaking free for long rushing touchdowns, or pretty passing scores to my receivers, or kickoff or punt returns...

Coming off back-to-back championships entering the 7th grade it was neat to be playing at the next level. Though my school was a perennial loser, I figured that would change with me around. My new coach was great, but his tough guy routine wasn't half as good as his jokes. A fun, funny and kind guy, I could never take him too serious. But I liked him a lot. I respected him. He was good to me and my teammates and never did anything to overstep his boundaries with us.

I never had a coach I liked more. He was a good-hearted guy who was great with teenagers, but was not a head football coach. That didn't matter. He did his best and we had fun together with great two-way communication and mutual respect.

That being true... Our season opener was embarrassing. We were starving for some real coaching and showed up totally underprepared for the competition we faced. Our coaching was more general and open-ended. Coach was the main reason why. We were just fortunate to have great competitors on our team, and I was a running quarterback. That first game was sobering. Both front lines getting beat badly, but our offensive line was worse than our defensive line.

We lost the first two games by getting out-coached, outplayed and outclassed. We fought through and started coming together a little later than the other teams. Getting some game experience taught us more than we learned in practice. After losing the second game Coach said, "If you want to call a different play than I call. Go ahead! If you've got something better than my play, call it. Take charge out there. Be in command."

The last part I heard louder than the rest. He said it like, "Really now, I'm telling you. I mean it." He was giving me authority to take charge and be in command even if it meant overruling his play calling. He could use the help, I knew, but I tried not to change plays too often.

We were 0-2 and in last place, facing the school that won the championship the year before, on their field. I decided we needed to seize the day. I wasn't sure how, but I was serious. I wanted to win. I wanted to really compete, not get blown out again. It would be vindication to beat the best team. I kept talking in practice reminding everybody we had to be fearless. I wasn't used to losing and didn't want to lose again, but I couldn't win the game by myself.

Monday my teammates dismissed me. Tuesday a couple guys started getting on board. Let's do it. We'll shock 'em... I kept it up Wednesday saying they would be looking past us. We could catch them off guard. They were the best. We were the worst. They wouldn't play their best game. If we played our best we could win!

Thursday I said it all again. We needed to really "try to win" and this was the team to beat. It didn't sound possible except how good teams look past weaker teams. And weaker teams do feel vindicated when they beat better teams. It's one of those things about football. On any given Sunday... the worst can beat the best.

That Friday we were on their field. Last-place versus first-place, and it happened like I predicted. They were looking past us and were sloppy on offense. Can't say the same about their defense because they were phenomenal defensively. But on offense they stunk it up, committing penalties all game long. We played out of our minds on defense and I had my personal best game of the season defensively.

After taking the opening kickoff they crushed our offensive line the whole first half. We had some major help when they had two touchdowns called back due to penalties. It was 0-0 at halftime in a game of all-defensive highlights. I had my teammates believing at that point. We were tied with the best team. So I kept encouraging everybody saying we could win, don't give up. Believe. Dig deep. Fight for it!

Before the second half coach pulled me aside. "Line up anywhere you want on defense. Left, right, center... Wherever you want. You're 'F-R-E-E' safety, okay?" He said the last part with a chuckle. I grinned and went out to intimidate their quarterback and offensive unit by how I lined up and moved around like a wild man.

Nobody ever plays like that. Everybody has a real position. Imagine 10-guys in real positions and one guy doing whatever he wants? Under the circumstances it was a great idea, because it set me free to cover the entire field by myself. And I made more tackles that day than any game I ever played.

The third quarter was nothing but grit and grind. They scored again but had another penalty so it didn't count, and they lost 15-yards instead. By the 4th quarter it was still scoreless and we were still tied with the best team. What a slugfest!

Halfway through the last quarter it looked like one score would win the game. With time running out they drove down to inside our 10-yard line. We were playing on guts and heart, our best defensive game of the year. If we could stop them one more time... Maybe we wouldn't win, but a tie was better than losing again.

On third and goal I watched the quarterback break the huddle and look to one receiver then double-check the same receiver. When the quarterback took the snap I started drifting fast to the side of the field he'd been looking. He took a short drop, looked away, then back in the direction of the receiver I was keying on. My teammate was backing up to cover him as I headed over for support.

The pass was not a long throw, from about the 15-yard line to the back of the end zone, and it looked like the receiver might make the touchdown catch after he broke open behind me. But I could see I had a chance to maybe tip the ball off course. So I bolted over, jumped as high as I could, and reached to hopefully tip it away... But I didn't tip it. I caught it!

Interception!

Coming down was like slow motion as silence fell across the field sideline to sideline. Like everybody took a short breath, held it, and waited to see what was going to happen. When I landed, there was nothing but open field in front of me, and I was off in the blink of an eye. The crowd came back to life as I darted from our own end zone with everybody on defense reacting a step late.

Just like that, I had the ball with one man to beat, the quarterback who threw the interception. As I headed for the sideline he headed for me, but he didn't have a prayer. Nobody was catching me on my Pick-6 return for the go-ahead score as I sprinted the 105-yards to cross the goal 20-yards ahead of anybody trailing me.

Wham! Bam! Slam the door!

In a matter of seconds it was 6-0, with last-place beating first-place on their field at the end of the game! In front of their fans. Our fans went ballistic seeing us winning against the #1 team and the game almost over. Of course, it gave their coaches a collective heart attack and they were yelling and screaming. We didn't convert the extra point, but we had the lead with less than two-minutes to play.

They got the kickoff and made their fastest drive all day, right back to our goal line with just enough ticks left on the clock. Our unlikely victory was about to be snatched out of our hands. They were going to win the damn game after all... NO! NO! NO!

After we stuffed two running plays and left them with 3rd and goal at the 5-yard line, their next play unfolded like déjà' vu. As they ran the same play I intercepted before. I hustled over just like the first time, only this time the quarterback put more loft on the pass. I did the same thing again, and amazingly got high enough to barely get my fingertips on the nose of the ball. As unlikely as seemed possible, I managed to hang on and came down with it again.

Interception!

How I jumped that high can only be explained by sports science, but adrenaline had something to do with it I'm sure. Made me wish I could translate the motion to my high jump competition in track and field. The receiver had seen the same routine before, and reacted faster. Catching me coming out of the end zone from behind. But we ran out the clock and the ref blew his whistle. Game over!

I found out later their defense had held our offense to "negative total yards" rushing and passing. Talk about fun pulling that victory out of the air! My teammates were all over me celebrating going back to our bench. We were the only team to beat that team in their championship season.

Coming off the field I was noticing their cheer girls heading to the water fountains. Coach was cool with it, so I took off my shoulder pads and walked over to get a drink and talk to them. They were real friendly even though I'd just beaten their guys in a thriller.

We went on a winning streak after that game. Everybody thinking we were better than we were, including us. Believing in ourselves didn't hurt. One of my favorite highlights of the year came against the team that would end up finishing second. We were trailing when I called the play Coach sent in. Then I was walking to the line when I realized, huh-oh!

I couldn't remember the play.

I asked the fullback and he just looked at me. I asked the halfback and he told me the play but didn't say which direction. I looked at our formation and couldn't figure it out. My mind was racing. I couldn't just stand there... Looking around and thinking of calling time out, I saw their linebackers suddenly split wide in response to our set. Creating a huge open area just beyond the line of scrimmage in the middle of the field.

The down linemen were parted left and right, the linebackers were spread wide with no middle linebacker. It looked like some kind of mistake. I don't know what defense they were in, but there was nobody in the middle of the field beyond the line of scrimmage. If I could get past the line it looked like I had an easy 20-yard quarterback sneak.

We were near our own 30 and I was out of time so I called the snap count, got the ball and ran a quarterback sneak without calling an audible first. The linemen crashed into each other as I tucked the ball and ran across the line into the defensive backfield. Some of their defenders were so shocked they froze in place.

I picked up 10-, 15-, 20-yards before any tackler could get to me. Put a move on a defensive back and broke free for 25-, 30-, 35-yards. I was almost 40-yards downfield threatening to go ALL... THE... WAY! But I didn't quite break the last tackle. It was the longest quarterback sneak I ever ran.

I had also learned to run like a mean terror. My dad had me watch Jim Brown replays where he hit defensive players to knock them off. So, I didn't always run from tacklers. But instead, often ran with the intention of hurting them if I could. Punishing the tacklers whenever I got the chance when I carried the ball.

"Don't take the hits," dad said. "Deliver them." When you can't escape a tackle and get away... Surprise-attack the defender instead. And some of my hits on would-be tacklers were just brutal. I got where I timed the hits, so right before a tackler "thought" he would intersect my path and hit me. I'd switch the ball and summon my strength and momentum to hit the tackler with my forearm or elbow first. Instead of just letting them hit me.

SMASHMOUTH running is what it was. Whenever I could tell there was no way to outrun them or fake them. Whenever they had the advantage and I couldn't avoid contact. That's when I would start headhunting, like I saw Jim Brown play. Change the timing of the collision and hit the defender, then spin away and try to break the tackle and be gone. I hurt guys I know, but never delivered a harder hit than in our last game that season.

It was after I had minor knee surgery to clean out loose cartilage in my right knee. Our final home game, and coach called a flat pass play just before the game ended. How ridiculous, I was thinking. Why? I looked to the sideline and hunched my shoulders at Coach, turning my palms up like, "What?"

The game was almost over and he called the perfectly worst play I could run. We should have taken a snap and dropped to one knee a couple times to run out the clock. I don't remember why I didn't change the play, but I didn't. I should have overruled him and run the ball. But I lined up and ran the play he called instead.

My mistake…

As the ball was coming out of my hand, I could see the cornerback had read the play. As I released the pass the cornerback was breaking to it already. I couldn't believe what I was watching as it happened right before my eyes. The guy stepped in front of my receiver, snatched my pass and headed for the winning score. NO, NO, NO! If he was going to beat me, I was going to make him pay.

It was about a 50-yard dash to the end zone. When I caught him at the 1-yard line, knowing I couldn't stop him from crossing the goal line. I lifted him off the ground in a two-part motion, so I could put all my energy into a down-ward THRUST with my shoulder and our combined body weight. It worked just like I wanted, as I bore my shoulder into him at the instant we hit the ground together.

There was a loud C-R-A-C-K and he screamed! His collarbone snapped on impact as I crushed him into the ground. I got up and stood over him watching him writhe in pain. His trainers came running up so I had to step out of the way. Then a lady ran over yelling and shaking her finger at me, so I walked back to my teammates.

I didn't care if they saw me crying, I was so furious at Coach for calling that play. And madder at myself for not changing it… I felt embarrassed for losing the game. Could we finish the season any worse? I couldn't believe what I did.

My teammates kept saying it was okay, I was the reason we'd won all the other games. I scored almost every touchdown all season, they reminded me. Don't worry about it, they kept saying. But I couldn't forgive myself that easily.

Multi-Threat Highlights & History

Michael Vick

Youth

Born in Newport, News, Virginia, Michael Vick was the second of four children. Living in a financially depressed and crime-afflicted neighborhood was not the kind of lifestyle Michael's father had in mind. Considering sports as a way out for his son, Vick's father started teaching him football skills when he was only three years old.

Vick learned more of the basics of the game from his second cousin, Aaron Brooks who played quarterback for the NFL Oakland Raiders in 2006. Oddly, the first time he picked up a football he used his left hand though he did everything else with his right.

At the age of 13, Vick stayed in touch with Brooks and worked with his coach James "Poo" Johnson to learn more about the game. He had already shown great potential in basketball and baseball in junior high, but chose to give up all other sports in favor of football. Aware of his strengths, the young multi-talented athlete modeled his game after Steve Young who was also left handed and had a strong arm and quick feet.

High School

In high school Vick rose to prominence in the early 90's. His natural skills for the game as a freshman at Homer L. Ferguson High prompted many to consider him a potential future star.

In 1996, Ferguson High School was closed, so Vick and his coach Tommy Reamon moved to Warwick High School. Upon taking over the role as coach of Warwick Reamon encouraged Vick to continue his development. In his first JV year as a sophomore Vick threw for 20 touchdowns.

Meanwhile, Warwick's varsity was struggling and searching for their X-factor. In a controversial decision, Reamon moved his starting quarterback to wide receiver and promoted Vick to varsity. The gamble paid off in Vick's second start, when he threw for 433 yards on just 13 completions.

Over the next three years, Vick's reputation grew and Reamon worked hard to refine the young quarterback's game. Vick was a three-year starter for the Warwick Raiders and in that time, passed for 4,846 yards with 43 touchdowns. He also had 1,048 yards and 18 scores on the ground.

As a senior, he passed for 1,688 yards, accounting for ten passing and ten rushing touchdowns. Running for six TDs and throwing for another three during just one game, he entered his senior season, as a SuperPrep and PrepStar All-American. By the end of his senior year, Vick had proven to be a playmaker as college coaches all across the nation sought his commitment.

College

It was a choice between Syracuse and Virginia Tech and the he chose the latter as his high school coach believed that under the tutelage of Frank Beamer at Virginia Tech, Vick would develop better. In the summer of 1998, Vick arrived at Virginia Tech's campus in Blacksburg and joined a talented recruiting class that included the likes of running back Lee Suggs and linebacker Jake Houseright.

Although Beamer gave Vick some action during preseason, he planted the new recruit on the sidelines once the regular campaign kicked off. In the 1999 preseason, Vick impressed with 4.33 time in the 40-yard dash, and a vertical leap of 40 and ½ inches, both school records for a quarterback.

Due to such strong performances, Beamer made him the starting quarterback in the fall of 1999. In his first collegiate game as a redshirt freshman in 1999, Vick scored three rushing TD's in just over a quarter of play. During the season, Vick led a last-minute game-winning drive against West Virginia in the annual Black Diamond Trophy game as the Hokies registered an undefeated season that resulted in an appearance in the Nokia Sugar Bowl national title game against Florida State.

His strong performances might not have handed his team the title but it probably helped earn Vick a cover spread of an "ESPN The Magazine" issue. During that year, Vick led the NCAA in passing efficiency with a 180.4 rating, which was a record for a freshman and the third-highest all-time mark.

His performances landed him an ESPY Award for the nation's top college player and the first-ever Archie Griffin Award as college football's most valuable player. He was also invited to the 1999 Heisman Trophy presentation where he finished third in the voting and matched the highest finish ever by a freshman at that time.

The 2000 preseason saw Vick work extremely hard to improve further on his prior year's performances. Vick was rejoined by Andrae Harrison whom he used to play with at Warwick High. The first three games of the 2000 campaign were scheduled to take place within a span of 11 days. Virginia's opener against Georgia was cancelled due to severe weather but the second game saw Virginia give Akron a 52-point thrashing.

The Hokies steamrolled past their opponents in the first six games, averaging 45 points a game. Ending the year with three straight wins, including a three-TD victory over Clemson in the Gator Bowl. In a game, Vick threw for one score, ran for another and was named the MVP of the game.

He completed 87 of his 161 passes for 1,234 yards with eight TDs and rushed 104 times for 607 yards. As his sophomore chapter drew to a close, Vick had to make a life-changing decision – whether to continue playing college football or move up to the NFL where it appeared he would be a first-round pick.

The decision wasn't easy, but Vick decided to forego the final two years of college eligibility. During his time at Virginia Tech, Vick made 235 rushing attempts, gaining 1299 rushing yards with an average of 5.5 rushing yards per carry, and 17 rushing touchdowns.

Pros

His decision resulted in pro scouts log a lot of overtime. Under most circumstances, a 20-year-old QB with around 300 throws under his belt would never come anywhere near the NFL radar screen. However, Vick had the intangible multifaceted skill that put him in a category of his own, as a genuine dual running and passing threat.

The weeks leading up to the draft Vick surrounded himself with a hand-picked group of advisors. At his Pro Day workout he ran the 40-yard dash in just 4.33 seconds and was later selected first in the 2001 NFL Draft by the Atlanta Falcons as he became the first African-American quarterback to be taken with the top pick.

The number-one selection belonged to the San Diego Chargers but they traded it to Atlanta Falcons the day before the draft for the Falcons' first and third round picks in 2001. Vick was also taken in the 30th round of the 2000 Major League Baseball Draft by the Colorado Rockies despite not playing the game since the 8th grade.

When Atlanta tied Michael down to a six-year contract worth a potential $62 million, including a signing bonus of $15 million, it was heralded as a major step towards a new era for the franchise.

Surprisingly, the Falcons did not intend to rush Vick. Coach Dan Reeves had plenty of experience when it came to mentoring talented young quarterbacks, having worked with the likes of Roger Staubach. Reeves knew from the start that Vick had extraordinary talent and leadership qualities, but refused to start him.

In the 2001 regular season, Reeves went with Chris Chandler as his starting quarterback and made Vick ride the bench and watch from the sideline. However, the rookie's performances in the training camp were so mind-blowing that the coaching staff decided to start giving him some real action every now and then.

In September, Vick completed his first NFL pass to wide receiver Tony Martins in the second quarter against the Carolina Panthers. In the same game, he scored his first NFL touchdown on a two-yard rush in the fourth quarter and the Falcons got the 24-16 win. Vick made his first start against the Dallas Cowboys in November throwing his first touchdown pass and winning the game 20-13.

In the season finale against the St. Louis Rams, he accounted for 234 of his team's 255 yards and ended his first season in the NFL with two starts, eight total games played. He completed 50 of 113 passes for 785 yards with 2 TDs and three interceptions. He rushed 29 times for 289 yards and one touchdown.

The 2002 campaign saw Vick playing more regularly in 15 starts. He completed 231 of 421 passes for 2,936 yards and 16TDs, had 113 carries for 777 yards and eight rushing touchdowns and also set a then-NFL record for most rushing yards by a quarterback in a single game with 173 against the Minnesota Vikings. He had a streak of 177 passes without an interception as the Falcons finished with a 9-6-1 win-loss record and the franchise got into the playoffs.

It was the breakthrough season Vick, in which he made one jaw-dropping 44-yard touchdown run against the Panthers, not to mention a 40-yard against-the-grain bullet versus the Green Bay Packers, which became the lead of a November 2002 story in USA Today Sports Weekly.

During that same season, he went longer than any quarterback, before throwing his first interception. On January 1, 2003, Vick helped the Falcons romp to a 27-7 upset victory over the favored Green Bay Packers in the first round of the playoffs. After the National Football Conference divisional playoff game, Vick was named to his first Pro Bowl.

In the 2004 regular season, Vick passed for 2,313 yards with 14TDs and 12 interceptions. He rushed for 902 yards and three TDs and in a game against the Denver Broncos, becoming the first quarterback to throw for more than 250 yards and rush for over 100 yards in the same game. He also set an NFL postseason QB record with 119 rushing yards in the first round of the 2004 NFL playoffs.

He was named to his second Pro Bowl after a season in which Atlanta won their third division title. In the 2005 season, Vick passed for 2,412 yards and 16 TDs while rushing for 597 rushing yards and six TDs. He was again named in the Pro Bowl after the season. In 2006, he became the first QB to rush for over 1000 yards in a single season and also set a record by rushing for 8.4 yards per carry.

In the 2006 regular season, Vick set a single-season quarterback rushing record with 1,039 yards. During his five years with the Atlanta Falcons, he averaged 52.1 rushing yards per game, 7.1 rushing attempts per game, for a total of 529 rushing attempts that gained 3,859 yards and 21 rushing touchdowns.

During his time with the Falcons, Vick had proved himself a versatile quarterback and excellent scrambler not easy to defend. Moreover, his ability to read defenses helped his team a lot. He also showed an uncanny ability to lay the ball away from the defenders on his deep tosses.

On August 2009, Vick signed a one-year contract with the Philadelphia Eagles and in week 13 of the 2009 season, threw a touchdown and ran for one. After Kevin Kolb suffered a concussion in September 2010, Vick was given a start and he led the Eagles to a 28-3 victory. In that game, he threw for 291 yards and three TDs and rushed for another TD. He was named the NFC Offensive Player of the Month for September.

In 2011, he was named NFL Comeback Player of the Year and won the Bert Bell award. Vick also became the NFL's career leading rusher for quarterbacks in a game against the Buffalo Bulls, surpassing Randall Cunningham with a 53-yard scramble in the third quarter that gave him 4,946 yards rushing, surpassing Cunningham's mark of 4,928 yards. Coming into that game, Vick had already rushed for 228 yards on 32 carries, and became the first player in the history of NFL to throw for more than 400 yards and run for an additional 75 in the same game – in a game against San Francisco.

On February 11, 2013, the Eagles and Vick agreed to a one-year restructured contract worth up to $10 million. The next year however, Vick signed a one-year $5 million contract with the New York Jets and after initially choosing to wear #8 as a tribute to Steve Young, decided to change it to number 1, being the first quarterback in team history to wear that number.

5

PERKS OF THE GAME

When I talked to the girls in front of those coaches after my Pick-6 interception that won the game, I ticked the coaches off good. My two interceptions to steal that game were bad enough, but hanging with their cheer girls was more than the coaches could handle. I saw them staring me down. But my attitude was, "Hey, didn't we just whip your butts?"

To the winner go the spoils.

I earned the right to talk to whomever I wanted. Their coaching staff could just deal with it. The girl I liked at our school wasn't on the cheer squad and wasn't at the game. Her family was moving to New Orleans before Thanksgiving. But seeing the #1 team play together like they did, and meeting some of their girls, made me wish I went to their school.

Be careful what you wish for…

Surprise, surprise! Before I got to really make that wish, it was granted. And no, that wasn't all good for me! My father wanted me to play my 8th grade football at the other school. Fine, okay about the girls. Sure… But what about those coaches I pissed off?

After my first practice with my new team, I made dad stop the car so I could throw up. The coaches remembered me. Oh yea, they remembered me alright. And they ran my ass into the ground that first day of practice. Payback. It was my baptism into their discipline and hard work, with a little extra over-challenging for me. But I passed the test and the coaches acknowledged my talents.

That actually kind of worked the wrong direction for me ultimately. Like Cam Newton running circles around his older brothers and their friends as a kid, till he was moved up to varsity as a freshman in High School thanks to his raw speed and agility. Anybody could see what a danger my raw speed and agility posed. Just give me the ball and let me go!

Give me enough touches, and I'd give you enough touchdowns. My new coach said he wanted me switching to tailback to give me the touches, since the offense was built around a tailback carrying the load.

I felt honored, but I was a running "quarterback," not a tailback. So I questioned the logic of the move because it took away my freedom to be unpredictable as a running passer. Coach said I could switch back mid-season if I wanted. Just try it for a while first. So, I said okay. Plus, it sounded fun knowing my coach wanted me getting the touches. And it would help my new team win their second of back-to-back championships. So that's exactly what we did.

We ran over everybody we faced. Winning most games by halftime, dominating with our running game. I got the touches and scored the touchdowns. We had to earn it, but we had the best team. Undefeated and undefeatable is how it felt, and was.

Coach kept his word and let me play quarterback at mid-season. It was one of my best games individually. Playing quarterback came natural to me. I was a quarterback. Getting to play the position again made me want to finish the season at quarterback. But Coach went over my rushing stats and suggested I consider returning to my real position of quarterback the following season, when I started high school.

But my one game at quarterback that year was memorable. Getting to be at the helm again leading my team, playing the position I loved most. Running quarterback!

Though I always remembered the details of another day the week after that game, more than what happened in the game itself.

Football practice was unexpectedly cancelled one day the following week, which never happened. I can't remember why it did, but my ride home wasn't coming for 2-hours and I was stuck at school. Bummer. I decided to walk across the street to the convenience store, but on the way ran into my algebra teacher carrying a bunch of books and papers in her arms.

I said hi, and went to open the door to the breezeway at the front of the school.

One of the younger teachers on campus, we formed a friendship in the first month at my new school. Flirting casually and enjoying each other's comebacks... It was nothing but fun. I was learning. She was the teacher. It was math. But she would encourage my artistic side too. More like an English teacher than a math teacher.

"Are you free for a minute to help me?" she asked, stumbling with her armload. I said yes my ride wasn't coming for 2-hours, and took all the books from her. I thought we were going to her car, but when she walked to the side street instead, looked both ways and started crossing. I asked, "Where is your car?"

She laughed, "I'm sorry. I'm not going to my car. I'm going to my apartment. I live across the street here." We stepped up the curb and walked down the sidewalk to where it turned into the heart of the complex. Walking in her door, my teacher's private world opened before me.

She led me past the kitchen, through the den area and back to the dining room. Where I put the books on her dining table. Thanking me as she led me back to the door, she spun around suddenly with a sparkle in her eyes I wasn't expecting.

"You shouldn't leave yet," she said lightly with a smile. "You need to stay... You don't have anywhere to go, and I need to talk to you."

"Well..." I said, eyeing left and right without moving my head.

"Sit down, and relax and I'll get you something to drink." She directed me to her sofa saying, "I want to ask you some questions. I need to talk to you." So I sat down on her couch.

"Would you like some iced tea?" she asked walking to the kitchen. "Yes," I said checking out her place.

"SUGAR?" she said loudly from the kitchen.

"Yes, two spoons," I answered, musing at being in my teacher's apartment.

A moment later she came out and handed me a glass of iced tea, then excused herself saying she'd be right back before going to her bedroom. I was feeling a bit apprehensive sitting there, but it was all cool. What else was there to do?

Coming back in, I saw she'd changed into blue jeans and a white button-up shirt that was un-tucked, unbuttoned pretty low and she was barefoot. The room started feeling really warm when she pulled a desk chair over and sat across the coffee table from me.

"Relax... There's nothing to worry about. I need to talk to you. I want to ask you some questions."

I had never seen her dress like that, but it suited her personality. She was thin, but attractive and being more animated than in class. It was hard to not notice her shirt jiggle when she moved, and I didn't think she was wearing a bra. As she talked, smiling and being fun, I was nervous at first but gradually started to relax. As uneasy as I felt, the conversation helped me calm down till we were just enjoying each other's company. She was a neat lady. I really liked her. There was nothing better to do at school.

We talked close to an hour over two tall glasses of iced tea for me. When she got up, walked around the coffee table and sat right next to me. Our faces were at the same level because I was leaning back in the pillows and she was shorter than me.

"Thank you for staying..." she said softly leaning her head against my shoulder so her hair touched my neck and cheek. "Nobody ever visits me here."

I thought about that for a second then said, "Heck, that's no good. This is such a nice place. You should have somebody over sometime…"

As I was speaking, she leaned her weight into me, bringing our faces closer together. I stopped in mid-sentence and looked in her eyes, bright blue and gleaming into mine.

"We can go to my room," she whispered seductively.

I said, I said…

I said, "What?"

Completely flabbergasted, I could hardly get the question out. My mind short-circuiting because I could hear her just fine, but I wasn't sure she said, or meant to say… Then she said it again.

"We can go to my room. If you want to?"

Sitting up quickly I gathered myself, "Maybe I better go now." She said no, I couldn't leave yet. But I got up and walked around the couch to go to the door. As she headed me off in the other direction. We met on the other side of her sofa facing each other. Saying nothing we stood there, her blocking my path to the door, me blocking her path to the bedroom.

"Don't leave," she said stepping up, slipping her arms around my waist and pulling up against me. I stood still and erect. Neither of us moved for a minute, but I could feel her breath on my neck and her breasts were warm and soft against me.

"I guess I better go…" I said again.

She looked up without letting go, paused then said, "I saw you play quarterback last week… Did you see me?"

Young athletes generating attention in sports can find themselves facing all kinds of challenges they never expected to experience. Walking briskly back to school after we finished, I was out of breath and my heart was racing like I'd escaped a tackle and scored a long touchdown.

Sometime later that season against another team, we had taken over on offense inside our own 5-yard line after a deep punt. They knocked us back a couple plays and we were hanging on from our own 1-yard line. It was third and long when Coach called a wide sweep-right to me. I was thinking, "Coach! You know better than that!" A sweep, from our own end zone?

I was wondering how I was supposed to not-get-tackled for a safety, when the quarterback took the snap and pitched me the ball. Darting to my right things shut down fast, so I spun back the other direction. But that was worse, so I turned back again with both sides converging on me.

With no chance of escaping and a major collision imminent I ducked low, put my hand on the ground to pivot and pushed off with my feet. Shooting out low to the side and back toward the field, I managed to escape the big pileup in a split second reaction. Hardly even getting touched as everybody crashed into each other where I had just been one-second before.

Keeping my balance, I looked up to find a wide-open field and I was off and running as fast as I could. Cranking it to full stride with only one defensive back to beat, but the guy was keeping up with me. I glanced back and he closed a step. Wow! Nobody kept up with me like that! But this guy was FAST !!

When I looked back in front of me a lanky gold dog came loping across the field, heading right into my path. His tongue flopping up and down as fans in the stands rumbled louder the closer I got to the dog. When I was about to need to juke the dog to avoid running into him, I changed strategies, kept running right at him and jumped him like a hurdler clearing a hurdle in track.

The crowd busted out laughing in their cheers! The guy behind me closed another step, and we ran the last 50-yards to the goal line together.

Touchdown!

Kids from the other team were clapping at the goal line, for my 100-plus yard "jump-over-a-dog" sprint and score! It was a play for the ages, with fans from both teams on both sides of the field celebrating at the same time. Not bad for a play that looked like a safety in our end zone at the start.

Like modern multi-threat playmakers, I could make something out of nothing with my instincts and my feet. My playmaking mindset helped me make great plays so I could be a difference-maker in games. A threat to take it all the way any play... My teammates knew it better than anybody. They knew me, and knew I was trying to break it every play I touched the ball.

It was great playing like that with coaches who worked us hard to help us be our best. We were a champion-hearted bunch of guys and we steamrolled over the other teams. My new offensive mates knew when I had the ball... if the whistle hadn't blown yet, I was on my feet trying to break it whether they could see me or not.

Those guys helped me be the eccentric threat I was on the football field.

They would stay in the play when the play got extended on sweeps or on cutbacks across the field. It was so cool faking defenders, breaking tackles and cutting on a dime to get past everybody. Then looking up to see one blocker catch up and lay out the last guy to pave the way for another score. That's how we played. We knew we could take it all the way any play. I didn't score all those touchdowns by myself.

And every time I crossed the goal line, I would either drop the ball like it was nothing special. Or pitch it to one of the guys who blocked to make it possible. No showboating. I never once spiked the ball after I scored. That wasn't me. When I see guys gyrating around and beating on their own chests it doesn't work for me. I'd bench a player for antics like that if I was their coach. Then take time to talk to him, to explain he's better than that. No need to overplay your part if it diminishes your teammates at all, by putting the focus on "yourself" after the whistle blows.

For what purpose? Or in other words, why do it? No, son... The play is over after the whistle blows. And there's no rule I know that says you're supposed to blow your own horn after the ref blows his whistle.

What you're supposed to do is run back to the huddle like your teammates and keep operating as one. Maintain that collective force of oneness and joint-willpower together. Maintain the team unity first, without dancing in the limelight of your own self-glory.

The play is over. There's nothing left to do. Get back to the huddle with your teammates and get ready for the next play. Stay in the moment. Don't bask in your own glow between plays. The game isn't over. The play is. Stay in the moment with your team.

Multi-Threat Highlights & History

Cam Newton

Youth

Born on May 11, 1989 in Savannah, Georgia, Cameron Jerrell Newton already had a taste for football, being the son of Cecil Newton who was an undersized linebacker for Savannah State in the early 1980s. He later tried out for Buffalo Bills and the Dallas Cowboys but didn't make either roster.

Eager to give his sons Cecil Jr. and Cameron an edge he never had, Cecil Sr. put both sons through college-level drills before they reached their teens. Cam Newton started playing organized football as soon as he was allowed and by the age of eight, was already showing signs of a great future ahead, and stood five-feet tall and weighed almost 100 pounds.

Since he was playing in a weight-based league, Newton often skipped meals in order to remain eligible. At age of 14, he enrolled at the Westlake High School where his phenomenal strength and athleticism for one so young quickly impressed coach Dallas Allen.

High School

Newton moved from the freshman squad to the varsity by the end of his first year. And after an older player broke his finger, he got a chance to start as a sophomore. Between his sophomore and junior seasons, as a 16-year-old junior, Newton passed for 2,500 yards and 23 touchdowns and ran for 638 yards and 9 TDs – performances that alerted major college programs.

He added three more inches to his height and 15 pounds of muscle to his weight. By his senior season, he could throw the ball 75 yards in the air and run over just about any tackler on the field. Due to his versatility, college recruiters who watched Westlake's games were divided over Newton's future position. Some thought that he should continue his development as an option quarterback while others felt that he had ability to become a good pocket passer. In his senior year,

Newton was rated a five-star prospect by Rivals.com, the second best dual-threat QB in the nation and the 28th overall. His performances led him to receive scholarship offers from Florida, Georgia, Maryland, Ole Miss, Mississippi State, Oklahoma and Virginia Tech. After much pondering, the young quarterback committed to the University of Florida at the beginning of his senior year in 2008.

College

Newton initially attended the University of Florida where he remained the member of Florida Gators football team in 2007 and 2008. As a freshman in 2007, the young QB beat freshman quarterback John Brantley as the back-up for future Heisman Trophy winner, Tim Tebow. In the five games he played, he passed for 40 yards on 5-of-10 and rushed 16 times for 103 yards and three touchdowns.

Just before the Gators' national championship win over Oklahoma, Newton announced his decision to transfer from Florida. In January 2009, the talented quarterback transferred to Blinn College in Brenham, Texas where he finally realized his true potential under the tutelage of head coach Brad Franchione, son of Dennis Franchione. Year 2009 was really productive and groundbreaking for Cam Newton. Throwing for 2,833 yards with 22 touchdowns and rushing for 655 yards, Newton was in full bloom and led his team to the 2009 NJCAA National Football Championship.

Rivals.com ranked him as the number one quarterback from either high school or junior college and he was also the only five-star recruit. He was named a Juco All-America honorable mention and was the most recruited Juco quarterback in the country. During Newton's recruitment, Oklahoma, Mississippi and Auburn were his three finalists and he eventually signed with the Tigers.

Newton started the first game of Auburn University's 2010 season, which was, a home win over Arkansas State on September 4, 2010. In his first game, he accounted for five offensive touchdowns and over 350 yards of total offense passing and running. Following his strong showing, he was named SEC Offensive Player of the Week.

A few weeks later, Newton had a second breakout game in which he registered five touchdowns and over 330 total offensive yards against the hapless South Carolina Gamecocks. On October 2, 2010, he helped Auburn to a 52-3 demolition of Louisiana-Monroe in a game he completed three touchdown passes, one of which went for 94 yards as the longest touchdown pass and offensive play in the university's history.

A week later, he led Auburn to a well-deserved win over Kentucky. In that game, he passed for 210 yards and rushed for 198 yards including 4 rushing touchdowns. When he ran for three TDs and passed for another one against Arkansas the media put the young QB in their Top-5 to watch for Heisman Trophy consideration.

On October 23, 2010, Cam Newton broke two records while leading Auburn to a 24-17 win over LSU Tigers. In that game, Jimmy Sidle's 40-year old record was broken when Cam rushed for 217 yards, giving him 1,077 yards for the season and setting the SEC record for yards rushing in a season by a quarterback.

The second record broken was Pat Sullivan's most touchdowns in a single season. A record that had stood since 1971. Both records were broken on the same play: A 49-yard touchdown run that saw Newton break and/or escape several tackles and by sheer strength drag a defender into the end zone for the touchdown. The play was described as Newton's Heisman moment.

After the game, the youngster received his first No. 1 overall BCS ranking and was listed as the overall favorite for the revered Heisman Trophy. In the halftime of the game against Georgia, Newton became the first SEC player to throw for 2000 yards and rush for 1000 yards in a single season. The win also handed Auburn the SEC West, paving the way to playing in the SEC Championship game against Alabama.

In the Iron Bowl, Newton led his team to a 28-27 win after the team initially went down 24-. The come from behind was the largest in the program's 117-year history. He passed for 216 yards with three passing TDs and ran for another. On December 4, 2014, Newton led the Tigers to their first SEC Championship since 2004. Newton was given the MVP award for the game he scored a career best six touchdowns.

He also became the third player in the NCAA FBS history to run and pass for 20-plus touchdowns in a single season. In the same year, he was named the SEC Offensive Player of the Year and the AP Player of the Year. He was also one of the four finalists for the Heisman Trophy that he won going away.

Cam Newton is only the third Auburn player to win the Heisman Trophy along with Pat Sullivan and Bo Jackson. In January 2011, Newton led his team to the BCS National Championship title against the Oregon Ducks. During his successful sojourn with Auburn, the multi-talented QB registered 1473 rushing yards at 5.6 yards per attempt, accounting for 20 rushing touchdowns, with a pass completion percentage of 66% and 2854 passing yards.

Pros

By late January 2011, Newton had already begun working out with George Whitfield Jr. in San Diego. Whitfield had previously worked with Akili Smith and Ben Roethlisberger and knew the young QB had a clear shot at making it big in the NFL. On April 28, 211, Newton was selected with the first overall pick in the 2011 NFL Draft by the Carolina Panthers and became the first reigning Heisman Trophy winner since Carson Palmer (2003) to go first overall.

He was also Auburn's fourth No. 1 selection. During the 2011 NFL lockout, Newton spent more than 12 hours a day at the IMG Madden Football Academy in Bradenton FL, spending around two hours a day doing one-on-one training with fellow Heisman Trophy winner and ex-Panthers QB Chris Weinke.

On July 9, 2011, Newton signed a four-year deal worth over $22 million with the Carolina Panthers. Newton decided to keep the #1 jersey that the Panthers had assigned him after the draft. With the body of a linebacker and the speed and quickness of a tailback, Newton had everything in his arsenal to hit the NFL with all the subtlety of a head-slap. Unlike most quarterbacks who come to the league, Newton already had a powerful arm, the quick feet and decision-making to go with his unwavering confidence to help him make Carolina's drop-back passing game work.

Newton's debut for the Panthers was nothing short of extraordinary. In the game against the Arizona Cardinals, he was 24-37 passing for 422 yards, and 2 touchdowns with a QB rating of 110.4. He also delivered with his running skills with a rushing touchdown, and became the first rookie to throw for 400+ yards in his first NFL game.

His 422 passing yards broke Peyton Manning's rookie record for most passing yards on opening day. In his second career game, His 854 passing yards in his first two games were the most in league history by a rookie and broke the record previously held by Kurt Warner in the 2000 season.

He was also the only player to begin his career with consecutive 400-yard passing games. Cam threw for 256 yards and 1 touchdown in week 7 win over the Washington Redskins, completing 18 of 23 passes. He also rushed for 59 yards and a touchdown, including one game-breaking run of 25 yards.

That performance brought his QB passer rating to 127.5. Following the Panthers' win over Indianapolis Colts, Newton became the fourth rookie QB to pass for over 3,000 yards in his first season. In early December, he set the NFL rushing TD record for quarterbacks. Blowing the old QB model out of the water, futuristic QB Cam Newton rushed for his 13th touchdown of the season in the fourth quarter against Tampa Bay.

After strong performances all season he was named AP Offensive Rookie of the Year and Pepsi NFL Rookie of the Year, and heading to the Pro Bowl.

In his first 2012 game he completed 23 of 33 passes for 303 yards and one touchdown. A week later he went 14 for 20 for 253 yards and a touchdown and delivered with his running skills rushing for another 71 yards and another touchdown. Cam led his team to a 21-13 win over Redskins against the new man on the block, RG-III.

During the 2012 regular campaign, Newton improved in many statistical categories and cut back on his turnovers. Newton led the league in Yards per Completion. In week 3 he guided his team to a 38-0 win over the New York giants, going 15 for 27, for 223 yards and three touchdowns, and he made a 45-yard rushing touchdown.

Facing Minnesota a few weeks later he went 20 for 26, for 242 yards and three touchdowns, and ran 30 yards for another touchdown in a 35-10 win. Newton led his team to a 12-4 record and a first round bye in the Playoffs. He was also selected for the 2014 Pro Bowl and drafted 3rd in the first annual Pro Bowl Draft by Team Sanders.

Through 2013/2014, Newton boasted a pass completion percentage of 59.8, 64 passing TDs, 364 rushing attempts, gained 2032 rushing yards with 28 rushing touchdowns. He has averaged 42.3 rushing yards per game, gained 2065 yards from scrimmage and 28 rushing and receiving touchdown.

6

STRAIGHT & NARROW

Heading into my freshman year in high school, I knew before school started I would be lettering on the varsity track team. The head track coach had called me in and told me after an unofficial pre-season football practice. It was no secret I had just won 1st-place in the 100-yard dash at the summer regional finals for the state track meet.

Like Robert Griffin III, I brought uncommon speed with me in my bag of gifts and talents. But I almost didn't even place in the race I won, because I almost didn't run in the race. I showed up late for the start of the race thinking my heat was next, not the one I was watching the runners line up for... Jogging briskly toward the starting line I saw the sprinters get in their blocks. Getting closer I stopped to hear the guy call out the start of the race, then...

POW!

The runners all came out at once. Only, one of them had jumped the gun.

POW!

The starter fired his pistol again to signal false start. All the runners stopped and headed back to start over. I asked somebody what race it was, and they said it was the heat I was supposed to be in!

<PANIC ATTACK>

I ran quickly to the starter with the runners getting in their blocks again. I asked if it was my heat of the 100-yard dash and it was, so I said, "I'm in this race!" He asked my name and looked on his sheet then said, "Okay son, you can line up over there," and motioned to the farthest and only empty lane.

"But I don't have any blocks!"

"Son, we're about to run this race," the guy answered. "If you want to run in this race, get in your lane or get off the track!"

Hurrying over to the far lane I discovered it wasn't a lane at all! But half of a lane. I stood there with no blocks wondering if I should get down like I had invisible blocks. I'd never seen anything like it. My shoulders were almost as wide as the lane. I looked down the track, then over to the starter and dropped down like I had blocks.

"Runners to your marks. Get set..."

POW!

The race was on...

The 100-yard dash, or 100-meters these days, doesn't last very long. When you get out of the blocks, come upright and get going – you better get in the lead if you want to win. Because it's going to be over before you know it. At the same time, it can seem slow if you're one of the runners because it's not over in just a second or two.

Imagine running faster than you ever ran in your life, and you're in a race like this. Flying like the wind and it gets to the 3-second mark. Imagine it getting to the 4-second, 5-second marks. That all happens in 50-yards or less in a real race, when you reach that time on the timer's stopwatch and you're only halfway to the finish line.

After nearly missing the race completely, my adrenaline was pumping extra energy into my legs. I was the only runner with the distinct disadvantage of having to start without starting blocks. So everybody got out faster than I did. But not for long.

Not every sprinter has the same degree of quickness. Quickness and speed are not the same things. Most athletes have one or the other, not both. Even though the other guys beat me out of the blocks, I got to my top speed so quickly I was pulling even at 30-yards. Then reached the leaders by the half-way point and kept going. I got a half step on the guys in the lead at… 6-seconds, 7-seconds.

With less than 3-seconds left I had a stride on the closest challenger and held that lead till the tape broke across my chest. My fastest time running 100-yards at 9.8 and when you run that far in less than 10-seconds. You're fast!

I shocked everybody. One timekeeper said a different guy had a faster time. I looked at him like, are you an idiot or what? He kept arguing for the other sprinter. Then all the timekeepers overruled him and said there was no dispute. Nobody needed a stopwatch to see who won the race. One guy broke the tape at the finish line and that was, Me.

Though I placed first in the regional meet and earned a trip to the State Finals, I decided to go fishing in the Laguna Madre with friends and enjoy my summer instead. Dad got mad, but didn't force me to go to the meet. I already knew how fast I was and didn't feel like I needed to prove anything to anybody, and sports are over-emphasized enough in kids' lives. I wanted to do something else with my summer than try to impress people with stop-watches. And I made the right decision because we loaded the boat with redfish and trout the weekend the state finals were held in Dallas.

Before football season started the team was meeting for unofficial practices. We all ran the 40-yard dash, and some of us were asked to run a couple other distances. I was the fastest in all of them, though only a freshman.

Coming into that year, all I could think of was getting back to my real position. Running QB multi-threat playmaker! Like my coach said the year before, how I should think about playing quarterback again next year. Pumped and ready for the season to begin, I knew I'd be joining the varsity football team or JV, since I was already on the varsity track team a semester before track season even started.

But when school opened, I was on the "freshman" football team. Hmmm... I went to my new head coach and said there must be a mistake. I'm on the varsity track team. I can't play freshman football. I needed to at least be on the JV team, so they could move me up once they realized what I could do. I reminded my new coach that I was faster than any sophomore, junior or senior at our school.

He said no, I would be on the freshman football team. Hmmm... I didn't say anything at first. Then finally said, "I need to talk to the varsity coach, this isn't right. If I'm on varsity track, I should not be playing on the freshman football team."

Coach said, "It was the varsity coach's decision. But if you want to talk to him go ahead."

Unbelievably, I wasn't going to be on the varsity team, I wasn't going to be on the JV team... The morons were going to make me play freshman football. And a dark cloud of bitterness and anger came over me like a curse. I became surly and unfriendly at practice. Even if my teammates didn't realize I was having a meltdown, fury and wrath were in my veins. Every heartbeat was to the same rhythm in my soul. ANGER and FURY and RESENTMENT!

I was so mad I wouldn't speak to anybody, even if they didn't really notice the change. Players, coaches, teachers, other kids... I kept a rumbling grumbling private dialogue going all day long, cussing everything and everybody under my breath. Who were they to defy me? I was pissed.

I went to practice hating the arrangement. Then I got the next best, WORSE news! I would not be playing quarterback either. I would be playing tailback again. My tailback stats were too good to ignore. And my coaches couldn't see me doing anything else. I felt heartsick. None of them had seen me play multi-threat quarterback. They didn't know what I could do...

I became a sullen teammate as the season started. I'd show up game day and dazzle the crowd for everybody, but I wasn't impressed with myself knowing we were playing teams who raided their best JV and freshman players for their varsity or JV teams. Like our coaches should have done. It became a meaningless season to me. A waste of my time... They didn't deserve to have me on their team if they couldn't recognize my talent and skill level.

Not knowing what "entitlement" was, or how badly ENTITLED I was acting. I kept at it. Building my rage by the day as the season progressed. Until it got the best of me one time. It was during drills when I looked skyward snarled at my situation and said under my breath...

"God... Let me break my arm so I don't have to deal with this sh-- anymore."

A simple prayer. It was hard to believe a season could be so boring, they would make me play so far below my talent level and I just had to accept it. Then came the one game that was worth playing that season. Against my old teammates from the high school I would have been attending, if I hadn't moved. Where I would have been the quarterback not a tailback.

Game day we boarded our bus to drive across town. Did warm ups and were lining up for the opening kickoff when I was scanning their sideline to see if I recognized anybody. But the refs were in a hurry to get the game going so I had to pay attention to the kickoff.

It was long and deep. I caught it at the 5-yard line and headed "wedge left" to our blocking scheme side of the field. Crossing the 15... I suddenly bolted right with no blockers in front of me but the sideline in sight. I had caught everyone in mid-step thinking I'd be following my wedge the other way.

I crossed the 20-, 25-, 30-yard lines... Both teams had overplayed the wedge side of the field. I saw daylight to the right and ran for it.

It was a footrace to the right sideline... At about the 40-yard line things were closing fast, but I saw a seam under the defensive coverage. As I was getting close to the right sideline, I suddenly made a quick catapult-jump-maneuver back to my left. Dodging the tacklers who thought they were about to catch me, and quickly heading in the opposite direction.

Everybody seemed like they were playing at half-speed compared to me as I dashed back toward the left sideline at a new angle across the field, I reached the 40, 45... covering almost 50-yards running sideways and back, when at midfield with nowhere left to go. I stutter-stepped to make the defenders pause for a split second, then blasted straight into the closest tackler trying to cut me off.

Hitting him in the facemask with my forearm as hard as I could, I knocked him back on his feet. He was trying to grab me but I turned on the afterburners, and it was all over but the crying. Bye-bye!

Touchdown!

Right in front of my old team and all their cheer girls. A 95-yard kickoff return for a touchdown to start the game! That was fun!

We kicked off to them. They went three and out, and punted to us.

I caught the punt about our 20-yard line and headed straight up the field before breaking left and switching to an upright "float" for a few steps. Changing speed and running more upright in staggered strides I made all the defenders break down to try and stay with me.

When you make a pace change first, you get to see how everybody else reacts. If you have the speed to outrun everybody, you time how the defenders react to what you do, until the moment you put on that lightning quick "first-step burst" up to speed. Do it just right, and the defenders look like they're standing still watching.

Veering the last 40-yards to their sideline I ran away from everybody and crossed the goal line on their side of the field for another score.

Touchdown!

We were up 14-0. I had touched the ball twice and scored twice. We hadn't run a single offensive play. Two returns for roughly 175-yards and two touchdowns. We were running my old buddies off the field halfway through the quarter.

We kicked off to them. They went three and out, and punted to us. But this time they punted out of bounds so I couldn't make it 3-returns in a row. But two returns back-to-back wasn't bad.

Taking over at our 30-yard line we finally ran our first play from scrimmage. Coach called Booger-Right to me... A wide sweep with an armada of pulling blockers to lead the way, I took the pitch and started at about 75% speed with a little jitter in my step, like I was thinking about turning straight up the field at any moment.

The problem for the defenders covering me was my pace again. It was deceptive. I looked like I was running faster, when in reality I still had other gears I could shift into. And that's what I did. I got them thinking we were all running fast and they were stringing me out, and I couldn't get around them. What gave me the advantage was how quickly I could make my initial burst, and get up to FULL SPEED sprint.

I jitter-stepped one slower stride and the defenders slowed for a moment in response. And just like that, I was gone again. I got a step on everybody, nobody could catch me and our crowd got to cheer for a long time as I ran the distance to cross the goal line for the third time.

Touchdown!

Up 21-0 with the 1st quarter ending, I had touched the ball 3-times and scored 3-touchdowns.

We kicked off to them. They went three and out, and punted out of bounds again.

With 240-yards in three plays by the start of the 2nd quarter, our offense took over around our 35-yard line. Coach called a wide sweep left to me. I ran like I was going wide left then cut straight up through several defenders, hitting one and twisting another or two around with head fakes and pace changes. My secret weapon of initiating contact worked again and I broke the tackles and kept going. It was the element of surprise that always fooled them.

But I didn't quite have a step on anybody. And a guy got a piece of me and held on. I started hitting his arm with my fist, and kept hitting him till he let go. But he slowed me enough that everybody was catching up. Then I got blindsided and was about to go down, so I stuck my hand out to catch my fall to pivot and get away again. The next instant... SNAP!

I heard it right as I went down and my facemask smashed into the dirt. I knew something was wrong. How it happened, just wasn't right. I went from holding myself up by one arm to smashing face-first into the dirt instantly.

The pile moved off me and I saw why... It was an ugly compound fracture. A clean break in my right arm, a couple inches up from my right wrist. So instead of my arm sticking out straight when I held it out, it turned and went up in the air between my wrist and elbow at a 90-degree angle!

It was gruesome looking, but the bones didn't break the skin so it wasn't bloody. Yikes! I got to my feet, took my misshapen wing in my other hand and trotted casually to the sideline. I wouldn't be scoring any more touchdowns that day! A new reality had arrived for me. And someone was sent to find my parents, I was told.

Standing there waiting while talking to my teammates, I noticed some commotion behind us then saw it was three of my former girl friends from my old school. They had come over to check on me. They were real sweet, it was cool getting to see them again and I was trying to talk them into getting me a ride to an emergency room when my parents showed up.

I picked up another 30-yards before I broke my arm on that last play. Finishing with just under 300-yards and 3-touchdowns in only 4-touches. Next thing I knew, I was out of football taking prescription painkillers for a severe compound fracture. And the worst part was... I asked for it.

Yep, and I knew it too. I got what I asked for, ugh. I couldn't help but remember my little prayer at practice. That was the worst part. It really messed with my head having that stupid prayer answered at such an inopportune time. I mean, what was God thinking?

Long after the worst of the pain subsided I still had my mom getting me pain pills for the "pain." It wasn't like I had planned to get hooked on painkillers. They just brought this pleasant euphoric groove that made me feel good. Quite innocently, I learned what its like to develop an addiction to prescription painkillers from a sports injury.

Eventually, I decided to go talk to my counselor privately about my new habit. But when she started asking pointed questions, I beat around the bush and wouldn't really tell her. She said I needed to pinpoint what I could change and take specific actions. I already knew that, but I had an involuntary craving for the prescription meds too, and didn't really want to stop taking them.

Walking out of her office I was thinking, that was a waste of time. When, I kid you not. Literally, this is true.

I looked up and crossing the main hall in front of the main entrance was my counselor's daughter. And she was coming over to me with a big smile on her face. Getting closer she came right up to me and said, "Hey there handsome," in a very uninhibited sexy way. She came closer and took my hand in hers, passing something from her hand into mine.

"Take it in quarters, it'll last longer," she whispered quickly. Then stepped back and continued talking like nothing had happened.

I was caught totally off guard but acted cordial, while wondering what the heck she put in my hand. The whole thing kind of overpowered my senses. Touching body to body like that in the hall. Putting something in my hand in front of everybody, but in a way nobody noticed. Acting like we were close with each other. It was all quite bewildering.

Not having the slightest idea what was in my closed fist, I got out of the crowd where nobody could see and looked in my palm to find six little orange pills wrapped in plastic. With a tiny note that read: Orange Sunshine! My hand clinched shut real fast and I looked up like I was guilty of something.

"Oh no!"

She must have seen me go into her mother's office I guessed, because she seemed to be waiting for me when I came out. That didn't explain how personal she was, but I did confirm later it was indeed 6-hits of LSD. And doing the math in my head, I realized how many trips that could add up to. I wanted to kick the prescription pills anyway and I was out of football for the rest of the season, so what the heck? It made sense. Really.

I couldn't play football. What difference would it make? Not the best logic ever, but I was young, immature and curious, with 6 pills x 4-quarters = 24 quarters. Or, 2-dozen "acid" highs! Wow! It would be a lot of tripping just getting rid of it. I was wondering how it might work as a painkiller, forgetting I wasn't really in pain anymore. That's how I transitioned from an innocent prescription drug habit, to a becoming a real-life LSD addict.

A kid on legal drugs one day. An addict on illegal drugs the next.

Rolling home with dilated eyes, seeing incredibly colorful things @#%$&*+ like I'd never seen before in my life. Streaking lights and colors, flying echoes of spoken words etched into the air like some floating holographic art… Laughing light-heartedly with my family like life was all-good. I realized I should probably go to my room. Where I could get my guitar out and calm myself before flying out the window into space.

Weeks later my new girl-friend gave me another six hits and I was totally strung out on LSD. Taking it all the time since it was free. I got the cast off, made it through the holidays and started preseason track workouts getting skinnier by the week. Until our first meet when I didn't break 11-flat in the 100-yard dash. One of my worst times ever, and my track coach wouldn't even look at me. I was hallucinating too even though I hadn't taken anything. It was getting bad.

I couldn't sleep in those days, so I would take more of my illegal medicine to keep going. It became my living hell 24-hours a day. I rarely came downstairs at home for very long because I was a walking bust. One look at me and anyone should have known. One day, my dad came in from work with a surprise.

Something to get me out of my funk he said. I looked at him through bedraggled bloodshot eyes.

He handed me a flat brown paper bag too thin to have much in it. I took the bag, looked inside and saw a piece of paper or something. Reaching in, I pulled out an 8x10 photo. Then I realized who it was and saw the personalized message under the image. I was speechless. It was from Roger Staubach! And the note said something like, "Good luck with your recovery. Come back even stronger!"

Come back even stronger? I couldn't speak at first.

My dad said, "How's that?" I was staring at the message not believing it was real. Good Lord, I was drugged out of my mind couldn't he tell? What the hell was he smiling like that for anyway? There wasn't anything stronger left in me. I was tripping when he gave it to me. But he was waiting for a response so I said thanks and went back to my room.

Later that night, I flushed the drugs down the toilet and decided to start my comeback. It was tough from the condition I was in. It didn't happen overnight either, but gradually I got clean and competitive again in my races. Like happened for strong man Samson of the Bible, it happened for me. As my curly locks grew longer during track season my strength came back, and with it my speed too.

With track season culminating in the District Meet that spring, I was looking forward to facing my arch rival one more time. A big strong brother who went on to be an NFL running back for the New York Giants. He'd beaten me every meet all season, but I got the better lane assignment finally and it's easier to gauge your opponent in the 220, (200 meters today), when he's lined up in front of you so you can see him ahead of you going around the curve in the first stage of the race.

When we got into our blocks and the race was about to start, I looked skyward and said, "Thank you." Then put my mind, body, spirit and soul into the moment. I had asked God for help getting off LSD and I had made it back to good health and full speed.

The starter shouted out, "Runners to your marks. Get set..."

POW!

We tore out of the blocks with spikes flashing and a ramped up fire inside to win the blue ribbon in the District Meet. Torching it around the top of the turn I passed him early. He was shocked and kicked into another gear as I did the same. We held through the turn...

Hitting the straightaway I was almost three strides ahead. He closed it to two strides early down the stretch and my heart was about to pound out of my chest. Not this time! He got a little closer and we held that separation. I never slowed down and he didn't gain another inch till the tape broke across my chest at the finish line.

WHAT A RACE! First and second place, stride for stride, and well in front of the other runners. We both had our fastest times of the season in that race!

Coming to a stop he walked over. "Great race, man! Great race!" And we walked back to the timekeepers catching our breaths and talking. He thought he was gonna' catch me. I said I thought so too! The only night meet of the year, it was cool having the cameras flashing as I won the race and when we were walking back together.

I had come full circle. From down and out to back on top! And yes, I sent a thank you message back to Roger for encouraging me right when I needed it most.

Multi-Threat Highlights & History

Robert Griffin III

Youth

Born February 12, 1990 in Okinawa, Japan, Robert Griffin III's parents were US Army sergeants who later moved to New Orleans, Louisiana. After settling at Copperas Cove, Texas, it was apparent the young athlete inherited the prowess of his dad, a high school basketball and track star during the early 1980s.

Griffin first gained athletic notoriety as a hurdler on the AAU track team coached by his father, winning a national championship in his age group. Despite his skills in track and field, Griffin always had a thing for football and modeled his game around John Elway, a player whose never-say-die attitude made an impact on RG-III.

High School

Slowly, his fame grew especially as a high school upperclassman when everyone started calling him RG-III. He played football, basketball and ran for the track team of Copperas Cove High School. As a junior, RG-III won the starting quarterback job for the Bulldogs coached by Jack Welch.

In 2006, he passed for more than 2,000 yards and had 25 touchdowns with only two interceptions. He also rushed for 876 yards and eight touchdowns, which led to First-Team All-District Honors. Apart from making it big on the gridiron, Griffin-III was making spectacular dunks on the hardwood and smashing state records in the hurdles.

After establishing new standards in the 100-meter and 300-meter hurdles, he was named Gatorade Texas Track and Field Athlete of the Year in 2007. His time in the 300 was .01 seconds off the US high school record.

College

RG-III graduated from high school a semester early after serving as class president and ranking seventh in his class. Despite his busy football schedule and being class president, RG-III had wrapped up all of his class requirements in the fall semester and started taking college classes.

During the college recruiting period, the young QB was pursued by Stanford, Tennessee, Kansas, Nebraska, Houston, Tulsa, Illinois, Washington State and Oregon. After initially committing to play for Houston under head coach Art Briles, Griffin changed his decision when Briles left Houston to take the head coaching position at Baylor. Griffin switched his commitment and signed a letter of intent to play for Baylor. Part of his reasoning in making the switch was the university's great track and field program.

As a member of the university's track and field team, Griffin finished first in the 400-meter hurdles at both the Big 12 Conference Championship and the NCAA Midwest Regional Championship meets. He also broke the NCAA Midwest Regional 400 meter hurdles record the same year. After placing third in the NCAA meet, the youngster participated in the U.S Olympic Trials and advanced to the semifinals.

RG-III graduated in three years with a bachelor's degree in political science and a 3.67 GPA. During his final year of college sports eligibility, he was studying for a master's degree in communications.

He earned the starting QB job for the Bears as a freshman, starting 11 of the Bears' 12 games that season. Lacking talent and playing in a tough Big 12, everyone expected Baylor to finish in the cellar of the 2008 South Division. But Baylor coaches knew they had a star in the making. In the young quarterback's performance against the Aggies he completed 13 of 23 passes for 2-TDs as the Bears won the game 41-21. RG-III completed passes for more than 2,000 yards and 15 touchdowns.

He also registered 843 rushing yards in the season and due to such solid performances, copped Big 12 Offensive Freshman of the Year honors. Griffin entered the 2011 campaign with great strength and confidence.

Thanks to his leadership, Baylor won seven of its first nine games and crept into the Top 25 national rankings that fall. The team scored four touchdowns or more in 10 of their first 11 games as RG-III made plays all over the field. The successful season earned Baylor their first Bowl bid since 1994.

They faced Illinois at Reliant Stadium in Houston, in the Texas Bowl and threw for over 300 yards in the game. That year, RG-III blossomed as a multi-threat talent, the likes of which Baylor had never seen. He completed 304 of 454 passes for 3,501 yards, for 22 touchdowns and was picked off only eight times.

He scored another eight touchdowns on the ground amassing 462 rushing yards. RG-III was First Team Academic All-Big 12, won the Manning Award, Davey O'Brien Award, was named Associated Press College Football Player of the Year and won the revered Heisman Trophy.

Pros

During his three seasons in college, most pro scouts thought RG-III might make a good NFL wide receiver. But his fourth season in Waco proved he was a genuine pro quarterback prospect.

Prior to his junior season, Griffin was not expected to be a first-round draft pick. But things had changed by midseason and he caught the attention of NFL scouts and analysts, with some predicting he would be an early first round selection.

Towards the end of his junior season, Griffin had established himself as the No. 2 QB prospect for the 2012 NFL Draft. The Washington Redskins selected Griffin No. 2, making him the second Baylor Bear to be drafted that high in four years and the first Baylor quarterback to be chosen second overall since Adrian Burk in 1950.

At Washington, he was surrounded with solid players, including receiver Pierre Garcon who was plucked off the Colts' roster during the summer. Upon signing a multimillion dollar deal with the Redskins, Griffin was allotted the number 10 jersey with Griffin-III written on its back and making him the first player in the history of the Big Four professional sports leagues to have a Roman numeral on the back of his jersey.

On September 9, 2012, RG-III became the NFL's first starting quarterback born in the 1990s. He showed a lot of promise when he took the field against New Orleans Saints in his official debut. The young quarterback completed 19 of 26 passes for 320 yards and 2 touchdowns adding 10 carries for 42 rushing yards, as Washington won the thriller 40-32.

He was named NFC Offensive Player of the Week, the first time in the history of NFL that a rookie QB was given such an honor on his debut game. His first TD pass as a pro was an 88-yarder to Garcon who hauled in a perfect throw at midfield and sprinted the rest of the way to pay dirt.

His was named NFL Rookie of the Week when Washington beat the Tampa Bay Buccaneers in Week 4. The start of October saw him named September's NFL Offensive Rookie of the Month. In his first game against the Minnesota Vikings, RG-III put on another incredible performance, including a 76-yard run for a touchdown. Griffin was named NFL Rookie of the Week for the third time in his young NFL career.

In mid-November, Griffin was voted by his team as the offensive co-captain and in the first game under this new role, the quarterback led the Redskins to a 31-6 win over the Philadelphia Eagles. He was named NFC Offensive Player of the Week for the second time. He had 200 passing yards with four touchdowns and rushed for more than 75 yards. His prowess against the Eagles made him the youngest player in NFL history to achieve a perfect passer rating in a game. In his first season, Griffin set records for the highest passer rating by a rookie quarterback (102.4) and highest touchdown to interception ratio (4:1).

Due to his phenomenal performances in his first-year campaign, Griffin was named to the 2013 Pro Bowl. In Week 7 of the 2013 regular season, Griffin helped his team to a tightly contested 45-41 victory over Chicago Bears. RG-III recorded 298 passing yards for two touchdowns including a 45-yard TD pass to Aldrick Robinson.

In their history, the Redskins may have had many fine leaders at quarterback. But when it comes to all-around football skills, Robert Griffin-III looks like the best leader since the days of Sammy Baugh. With a strong arm, great foot speed and excellent vision, RG-III is his team's mainstay.

Making accurate passes on the run and stretching out his time to throw by moving in the backfield gives Griffin-III the ability to limit mistakes, which is why he had the lowest interception percentage of any pro quarterback in 2012.

Griffin has a strong passing arm and can attack deep coverage. He has an easy, smooth throwing motion that shows little effort but the ball rockets out of his hand tight spirals and power. One can see a correlation in RG-III's early NFL play and that of Cam Newton in his rookie season.

The multi-talented quarterback made a major impact in his rookie year just like Newton did, with his uncanny ability to stretch the field and exploit deep coverage. As a former track and field star, Griffin is a dangerous runner when healthy. His speed and agility help him dart out of the pocket at crucial times to pick up first down yards.

Most mobile quarterbacks struggle when it comes to maintaining field vision as they lock in on defenders coming their way. Griffin is not a true drop back pocket passer, so his best opportunity to blossom in the NFL will require a coach like John Fox, who found success with Tim Tebow because Fox was willing to give the playbook a makeover to fit his unorthodox talents.

If Griffin gets to work with the right offensive coordinator from a new and improved, revised playbook designed around his strengths, he could really become a fun multi-threat talent to follow.

7

TUG OF WAR

I really liked my JV coach in 10th grade, and I did not like the varsity coach.

Coach Shane was head coach of the JV team, and we all respected him. Gave him all we had to give, and dominated in every way against our opponents. There was never any doubt in anybody's mind on the JV team. We had something nobody else had. We had agreement and a common will that was unmatchable. And Coach Shane was the catalyst of it all. He gave us freedom to play with all our hearts without having to bow down and kiss his feet first.

We hit it off right at the start, just having a mutual respect for each other and how we looked at the game. One thing he tuned into was my drive and force of will. Like Tim Tebow, I brought an intangible that is worth more than raw talent alone. I brought an indomitable will with my game. Which is why I respect Tebow's game. His will is something I wish I could bottle and sell.

Early in the year, when my pulling linemen were slow getting out wide to block, I got smothered HARD by a group of tacklers. I got back to the huddle and hit one of my linemen in the facemask, "F- YOU." Then hit another in the facemask and said the same thing to him. Everybody was going hey, hey... Huddle up! Huddle up! Another linemen walked over. I hit him in the face-mask and said, "F- YOU too!" When the last lineman came over like I better stop hitting people. I hit him in the facemask. "F- YOU too!"

And at that, "all-four" were pissed! They started surrounding me like I'd done something wrong. But what the hey! It wasn't me. It was them! I said, "I just got my ass buried in the ground because of you guys! Don't glare at me! GET OUT OF MY F'ing WAY!"

They were glowering at me so I said it louder: "GET OUT OF MY F'ing WAY! GET OUT OF MY F'ing WAY!" They closed the circle around me but I wasn't finished yet. "Where the F--- were YOU when I was getting GANG-TACKLED? Where the F--- were YOU?"

They were saying they were blocking but I said, "BULLSH-- NO YOU WEREN'T!"

Our teammates kept saying, ya'll stop it! Huddle up. I said, "I'm flying out there as fast as I can, and you guys are going half speed! HALF SPEED!" They denied it and kept making excuses. "I'm SEVEN-yards behind you, and you're on the line running ahead of me. HOW THE F--- AM I GETTING OUT THERE BEFORE YOU?"

They started getting madder as I kept pushing them. The quarterback was saying we had to run the next play. I said no, "We're running the same play again so we can get it right." Then I turned to my linemen again, "SHOW ME you're running fast, okay? SHOW ME!"

Our quarterback was arguing, "But Coach called a different play!"

"We're running the same play!" I said. "I'll tell Coach it was me." He finally gave in and we lined up to run the same play. Going to the line I was telling my blockers we could run over these guys, if they'd just get out faster! The defense was looking at us like we'd lost our minds. It was quite obvious we were fighting among ourselves. It was kind of funny because we had become a genuine distraction. The score was tied 14-14 and it was early in the 3rd quarter.

But when we ran the play again we picked up about 15-yards like a bulldozer had come onto the field. In one play we had them on their heels. Coach sent another play in and I stepped out of the huddle and waved it off.

"We're running it again." Nobody argued with me and we ran the same play for the third time in a row, picking up about 25-yards with the defense knowing what was coming. I remember walking back to the huddle laughing with my linemen as they were hitting me on the helmet and shoulder pads, and pushing me around. We were crushing their defense all of a sudden and having fun doing it!

They never scored again and we scored every time we got the ball the rest of the game until it was 48 to 14 and we notched another W into the stock of our gun. That's how it was all year playing for Coach Shane. We were a team that played together. A team that cared about each other. Invincible in our common will to deliver. And just as good as the varsity whenever Coach would put us up against them in practice. They had a much better passing game. We had a much better running game.

Whenever I broke free it was over, I was going to score. Nobody ever caught me when it was a footrace. I was one of the fastest teenagers in the state beyond my years. We went undefeated, also winning the two games when I didn't play because Coach had moved me up to varsity. But he never would play me in the varsity games except on defense at the end of the game.

As the season was ending and our defending "state champion" varsity team was about to make the playoffs. We were holding one of our last regular season practices when Coach ran with us to the lockers and gathered us just outside the door for a talk.

I was facing the field and saw our worst JV player finish his laps on the track across the field. Nice kid, but a sad story. Must have had a father forcing him to play. He'd been there for all the practices, and Coach Shane wouldn't force him to quit. But he couldn't play him either. The kid had paid his dues, but he would never be more than a third team player.

Coach Shane let him hang with us graciously. He'd been with us since the 8th grade when our old junior high coach would have us all run over and pile on him in the middle of a lap he was running. Yea, I got along with my coaches in 8th grade. But it was a matter of convenience. I got along with the head coach, but "Coach-a-bully" never realized how much I disrespected him for how he made us treat that kid.

Coach-a-bully would randomly yell out, "BONZAI!" Right in the middle of practice, out of the blue, and all the players would have to go pile on that kid together. I ran along but never piled on the guy. It didn't feel right to me. I didn't want to do it. Looking back, I wish I had gone to Coach and confronted him for making us mistreat a teammate.

Amazingly, the guy lasted as a freshman when I was hurt, and lasted almost all of his sophomore year. Until the day Coach was giving us that aggressive talk outside the door to the lockers and turned to see the kid staggering across the field after his laps, to go take a shower and go home. Coach flinched when he saw the exhausted kid stumbling his way across the football field.

Swinging his arms to clear us out of his way, Coach broke free from the circle of players and started running to the field. We were all wondering what he was doing, but nobody said a thing. The other coaches stood watching too.

Coach ran until he reached the track, ran across it and out onto the field on a beeline for that kid. The kid stopped and was just standing there. As the NFL struggles with admitting what it has allowed to go underexposed for years, their inept lack of policy for domestic violence and assault cases. I have to think more scrutiny needs to go WAY BACK DOWN THE LINE to the middle school and high school levels. Since football is a kid's game first, right?

As we watched, Coach ran up to the kid and leveled him. None of us could believe what we just saw. Coach mowed the poor kid down, then got on top of him and was straddling him as the kid lay on his back looking up. It was like a bad vision coming true that nobody wanted to see. Then he grabbed the kid's facemask raised his helmet and slammed his head into the ground. That motion real fast six or seven times in a row while yelling in the kid's face. Slam, slam, slam, slam, slam… he kept going.

It was shocking to see a grown man doing that to a kid who couldn't defend himself. It was so extremely unnecessary. Why not just tell the kid it wasn't going to work out. Why not be kind to him? What did he do to anybody? Wasn't he our teammate? Hadn't we let him stick around all season? Unbelievably, Coach did another series of slams with the poor kid's head and yelled some more at him. Then stopped, got off the kid and started walking back over to us breathing heavy.

That kid never came back after that day.

But the worst part was what it did to me. Because watching that ugly display of pitiful manhood and obnoxious bullying turned my heart against my coach. I felt hate that day. Young hate. Immature hate. I hated Coach after seeing him brutalize that kid like that. I didn't just disrespect him. I hated him. He should have been arrested before the sun went down. But instead, he got away with something no man should ever do to a young athlete.

I earned my way onto the varsity playoff roster by consistently defying the varsity defense in practice, and my amazing highlight playmaking in JV games. I was also a star punt and kick returner. The fastest man on our team, with some of the most natural multi-threat talents a coach could want a player to have. But the waters were troubled between Coach and me.

Coach hadn't let me really play with the varsity all season, so I wasn't expecting it when he deliberately set me up against his first team defense one more time. Like we had done all season on the practice squad, running over his defense... What was the point?

Coach Shane walked me away from everybody. He knew I should have been playing varsity all year. He knew I was worthy by my performance in all the JV wins. But I was getting one more chance to earn my ticket to play in the biggest game of the year for our defending state champion team as a sophomore.

No problem. I'd been a living highlight show all year. "You're getting plenty of carries this drive. Make it count," Coach Shane said. And I got his drift. This was my chance to win a nod for the semi-final playoff game in the Astrodome. Me against his starting playoff defense with lots of people watching.

Starting from our 20, we marched our JV offense all the way to their 10-yard line. And just like Coach Shane said, I got all the carries with the defense keying on me. It was fun running over them, around them and past them like that. We made it look easy, how fast we marched down the field. All on the ground without a single pass. All the way to pay dirt. Did they really think they were going to stop me?

The stage was set. The coaches were standing by to watch me score and impress everybody who was there that day. Coaches, parents, media and visitors watching us practice, with the semi-final game in Houston knocking at the door.

I took the pitch to run wide right and score. And when I scored... I would finally have Coach's respect as the best multi-threat running back on the team. My ticket to playing in the Astrodome, where I could show the world my game! My big chance to help my team win the semi-finals as a sophomore. Like I had won all the blue ribbons for our varsity track team as a freshman.

But that's when everything went wrong. That's when I stepped forward inside myself and said no more. No. This isn't right. I don't like this guy. And I don't like how he's coaching this team.

No disrespect meant to my teammates. No disrespect to myself. I meant to score and could have scored easily. But suddenly... the urge just left me. I wasn't trying to embarrass anyone. It wasn't premeditated. There was no forethought, but the unction just left me. It came out of nowhere and surprised me as much as anybody. If I had thought about it first, I wouldn't have done it. But it was a gut reaction.

It must have looked odd because I slowed before floating into the cornerback's arms. It looked like I just let him tackle me, which is exactly what I did. And he brought me down at the 2-yard line. Coach freaked! With all those people watching I'd shoved it right in his face. He ran over and yelled, "RUN IT AGAIN!"

Okay, okay... I'll run it again.

May not have been the best idea, at the best time. But maybe the worst idea, at the worst time. Regardless, I let Coach know I was playing for "my team," not for him. Period. He had failed to earn my respect and I didn't like the man. When you're an elite player, you cannot let a coach disrespect you. Even if you don't play because of how you challenge him. An elite player must show himself the respect he is due whether any coach does or not.

That weekend in Houston, we practiced in the empty dome the night before the big contest. Everybody was pumped. Coach had his secret weapon anytime he needed me. The fastest player on our roster. Possibly the fastest player on the field that night. He knew what I could do for my teammates. He'd been watching me all year. HE KNEW I was a team player who would deliver for my team. And he let me know he wanted to play me. Like I let him know I wanted to play.

But the nuances of the bad relationship... Good heavens! He wanted me to affirm his bullying ways and that just wasn't going to happen. I was glad to submit to our game plan and deliver for my team. But I would not affirm Coach's way of doing things. Team first, not Coach first. Sorry!

Win and go to the state playoffs! Lose and go home. Coach had a great team and a Wild Card on his sideline. A sophomore playmaker who could make plays and help bring home the bacon. The game was close, a toss-up at halftime. Then my divine moment arrived! When I would finally get to play at a critical moment in the game. To help save the day for my team.

Midway through the 3rd quarter the starting tailback got knocked out of the game. A great Herschel Walker-style runner, all north and south with no cutting. He was our state finalist hurdler from our track team. But he wasn't a multi-threat playmaker who could return punts and kickoffs for touchdowns like me. Everything was on the line, but instead of sending me into the game. Coach sent me in to help carry our starting tailback off the field.

When he needed me most and KNEW I could deliver for my team. He wouldn't play me. It boggled my mind, considering my season that year. My game after game heroics. What a mistake...

It only takes 1-play to make a difference in a game. And making plays was my forte! I was a game-changer. Give me a chance. Give me one play. Or one series. Our future NFL starting QB could have used some ground support that night. But Coach sent our 3rd-string tailback in instead of me, a small guy with no speed who wasn't an average running threat.

Playing for all the marbles! To reach the state finals for the second straight year! The reigning state champions! Coach knew I was the most explosive runner on our team. We had ridden our star quarterback's great arm this far, with his great receiving corp. But this was a playoff game against a better opponent. And our team needed somebody who could actually play tailback to get at least some yardage on the ground.

I went to our offensive coordinator. He walked away. I followed him. "Coach, I'll get it done, I promise." He turned and looked at me. He knew.

"Be ready when I call you," he said.

I stayed close to him through the 3rd quarter, and into the 4th quarter. But not even when we needed a 2-point conversion to win at the end would our head Coach agree to play me. Opting instead for a run-pass option, where he actually called a designed fumble into the end zone if the play didn't work. I heard it myself.

Time was running out in the game. They would win a tie to the tiebreaker-stats of the game. Our star QB leader took the snap, looked to throw or run, couldn't find anybody open and finally tried to run it himself. Great as his NFL stats prove he was, he was never known for his running skills, his elusiveness or his speed. He was known for his arm.

Unable to find an open receiver and stopped short of the goal line when he tried to run it, our QB fumbled the ball into the end zone and there was a mad scramble. Win and go to the state finals. Lose and go home. They recovered the ball. We lost and went home.

It made me sick to my stomach. Coach never played me a single down in that game. I was disgusted, not being able to help my team with what I did best. Coach should have played me. I could have helped us win the game and advance to the state finals. Even if I just helped pick up first downs and keep possession and didn't score.

I could have made at least 1-play to help us win, and go back to defend our State Championship for a possible back-to-back Championship repeat. I had led my teams to previous back-to-back championships before.

I was a playmaker. Elusive and fast… I could turn 1-play into a "W" / WIN.

We lost and went home.

Multi-Threat Highlights & History

Tim Tebow

Youth

Born on August 14, 1987 in Makati City in the Philippines to American parents who were Baptist missionaries, Tim Tebow was the youngest of five children. His mother, who instilled the family's Christian values and beliefs in him, also home schooled the future quarterback.

In 1996, after legislation was passed in Florida to allow home-schooled students to compete in high school sporting events, Tebow got the chance of playing football with on a school team. The law was later named the Tim Tebow law. The law allowed the youngster to attend the Trinity Christian Academy where he started playing as a tight end.

High School

In 2003, Tebow moved into an apartment in St. Johns County and was eligible to play for the below-par football program at Allen D. Neuse High School where he started playing as a quarterback. It was his running and throwing abilities, peppered with intense competitiveness that helped Tebow come into national prominence as a junior at Nease.

So great was his competitive drive that he played an entire second half of a game with a broken fibula and amazingly rushed for a 29-yard touchdown as well. Although the injury ruled him out for his junior season, Tebow's performances had done enough to earn him Florida's Player of the Year award and he was also considered a major college football quarterback prospect.

During his senior season, Tebow was the major force behind Nease Panthers state title. His performances throughout the season earned him All-State honors while he was named Florida's Mr. Football and a Parade magazine high school All-American and another Florida Player of the year award. He played in the 2006 U.S Army All-American Bowl in San Antonio, Texas, which featured 78 senior high school football players in the nation.

The game was shown nationally on NBC television. Tebow euphoria had gripped the nation so much he was the subject of an ESPN "Faces in Sports" documentary. The segment of the documentary was titled "Tim Tebow: The Chosen One" and focused on the Tim Tebow law, missionary work in the Philippines, his athletic ventures and the college recruiting process. The young QB was also featured in Sports Illustrated on the "Faces in the Crowd" page.

In 2007, he was named to FHSAA's All-Century Team that listed the Top 33 football players in the state of Florida's 100-year history of high school football.

College

Despite having family ties to the University of Florida where his parents had met as students, Tebow considered other schools, including the University of Alabama. In the end, it was the University of Florida he committed to. The major reason behind that was coach Urban Meyer's spread option offense, an offense for which Tebow was deemed archetypal as a quarterback.

Though he put in a strong showing in his first inter squad scrimmage, Urban Meyer named Tebow second string behind Chris Leak. Even then Tebow was a significant contributor to the Gators' 2006 success. He made his college debut coming off the bench in a goal line situation against Southern Miss. In that game, he rushed for a touchdown on a designed quarterback scramble on his first play.

In the next game against UCF he led the team in rushing yards. On September 16, Tebow made his SEC debut against the Tennessee Volunteers. Again, it was a promising display in which he had a ten-yard run on his first carry and converted a critical fourth down near the end of the game. Tebow's best however, came in the biggest game of the season against the LSU Tigers on

October 7 when he accounted for all three of the Gators' touchdowns, passing for two and rushing for another.

Later in the 2007 BCS National Championship Game, Tebow was again the star for the Gators as they beat Ohio State. That game saw the promising QB throw for one touchdown and rush for another while finishing with 39 rushing yards. He finished the 2006 season with the second most rushing yards on the Gators team.

The buildup to the 2007 season saw Tebow work more on his passing and due to great performances in the pre-season; he became the starting quarterback for the Gators. He opened the season with 13-of-17 for 300 yards and three touchdowns in his starting debut against the Western Kentucky University.

The regular season finished with Tebow boasting the second highest passing efficiency in the nation with 177.8. Moreover, he averaged 4.3 yards per carry on the ground. The 2007 season also saw Tim Tebow set numerous personal, school and national records.

University of Florida single-game quarterback rushing yards, 166

SEC season rushing touchdown record, 20

Career high single game rushing touchdowns, 5

SEC season total touchdowns passing and rushing, 55

In late November against the Florida State Seminoles, Tebow threw for three touchdowns and rushed for two in a 45-12 rout. What was amazing about his performance was that he had fractured his right hand during the 3rd quarter but played through the pain before sitting out the next three weeks.

Following a successful 2007 campaign, Tebow was recognized as a first team All-SEC selection and a consensus first team All American. For his outstanding performances on the gridiron, Tebow bagged the Heisman Trophy. He finished ahead of Arkansans' stalwart Darren McFadden, Hawaii's Colt Brennan and Missouri's Chase Daniel.

He was also the first sophomore to win the Heisman Trophy. He finished the regular season as the only player in the history of FBS to rush and pass for at least 20 touchdowns in both categories in the same season. He registered 32 passing touchdowns and 23 rushing touchdowns. Tebow's rushing TD total in the 2007 season is also the most recorded for any position in the history of the SEC.

The total also set the record for the most number of rushing touchdowns by a quarterback in the history of FBS. He also became the third UF player after Steve Spurrier and Danny Werffel to win the Heisman Trophy. He was the recipient of the Davey O'Brien Award, which is given annually to the best quarterback in the nation.

In order to get some workload off Tebow's shoulders, Florida coach Urban Meyer stated that he would likely use two quarterbacks for the 2008 campaign. On November 1, 2008 while playing against the Georgia Bulldogs, Tebow reached another milestone running for his 37th rushing touchdown and breaking the school record held by former running back Emmitt Smith. Tebow's sensational performances saw the Gators finish the 2008 campaign 12-1.

After clinching the Southeastern Conference Eastern Division title, the team qualified for and won the SEC title in the 2008 Championship Game against the Alabama Crimson Tide. With that win the Gators secured the #2 ranking in the final BCS standings. This earned them a clash with the #1 ranked Oklahoma Sooners in the 2009 BCS National Championship Game, which they won 24-14.

Tebow also won the Maxwell Award for the second time. Following the national championship celebration in January 2009, Tebow announced that he would not be making himself eligible for the 2009 NFL Draft and would instead return for his senior season at Florida. Tim Tebow carried his amazing success forward into the 2009 season with a streak of throwing and running for a touchdowns in blowout wins at the expense of Charleston Southern and Troy.

He ran for a touchdown in the third win against Tennessee. The 2009 season showcased the best of Tebow's competitive spirit and wearing-his-heart-on-his-sleeve will. Before the game against Kentucky, the youngster was suffering from a respiratory illness and had taken two bags of intravenous fluids. It wasn't enough to stop him, as he ran for two touchdowns to put his name second on the all-time SEC touchdown list. The QB ran for his 50th and 51st touchdowns playing against the Georgia Bulldogs and broke the SEC career record, which was previously held by running back Herschel Walker (Georgia). Tebow's final collegiate game was the 2009 SEC Championship game against the University of Alabama.

He threw for 245 yards and a touchdown and led the team with 63 yards rushing. In the 2010 Sugar Bowl in January, Florida beat Cincinnati 51-24 in Tebow's last college game. He completed 31 of 35 passes for 482 yards and three touchdowns and accounted for four total TDs and 533 yards of total offense which was a record for a Bowl Championship Series game.

Pros

Tebow entered the 2010 NFL Draft as a potential third round pick for the Jacksonville Jaguars, his hometown team. However, Tebow was selected by the Denver Broncos in the first round (25th overall) of the NFL Draft. He signed a five-year contract with the Broncos and on October 17, of his first year scored his first NFL touchdown on a five-yard running play against the New York Jets.

In the 49-29 home win over the Kansas City Chiefs, Tebow threw a three-yard touchdown pass to Spencer Larsen on his first career NFL pass attempt. He also added a one-yard rushing touchdown in the same game. Tebow started his first NFL game on December 19 against the Oakland Raiders, passing for 138 yards, including a 33-yard touchdown pass. He also rushed for 78 yards, 40 of which came on a touchdown run in the first quarter of the game. That was the longest touchdown run for a QB in the franchise's history and the longest touchdown run in NFL history for a QB in his first start.

In the 24-23 win over the Houston Texans on December 26, Tebow rallied his team from a 17-0 deficit at halftime and finished the game with 308 passing yards and one TD pass. Another rushing touchdown was added in the last quarter. Tebow finished his rookie season with a total of 654 yards, five TDs and three interceptions. He also rushed for 227 yards and six TD's and became the first QB in NFL history to rush for a touchdown in each of his first three career starts.

After beginning the 2011 season as a backup to Kyle Orton, Tebow eventually became the starter. Head coach John Fox's decision paid dividends. In the November matchup with the Oakland Raiders, Tebow rushed for 117 yards along with passing for 124 yards and two touchdowns as his team won the game.

Another win followed over the Kansas City Chiefs. Tebow completed two passes on eight attempts and a touchdown. His second completion was a 56-yard touchdown pass in the fourth quarter to wide receiver Eric Decker.

A few days later, Tebow was 9-for-20 in a Thursday Night Football game at home against the New York Jets. He led a 95-yard game winning touchdown drive in the last minutes of the 4th quarter and his team trailing. With last minute left on the clock Tebow ran the ball 20-yards for the final touchdown to win the game for the Broncos, 17-13. An unconventional QB kept finding ways with his teammates to win, and keep winning against all odds.

Tebow saved his best for the opening round of the playoffs, leading the (9-8) Broncos to a stunning win over the favored (13-3) Pittsburgh Steelers. On the first play of overtime Tebow completed an 80-yard touchdown pass to Demaryius Thomas, knocking the Steelers out of the playoff race and keeping Denver's Super Bowl aspirations alive.

Tebow completed 10 of 21 passes for 316-yards and a 31.6 yard per completion average. Coincidentally matching the white numbers he put in the black paint under his eyes at the University of Florida- John 3:16. It was another miracle-like victory by another Tebow-led team, this time in a highlight reel season. Where one NFL coach was willing to retool a pro playbook to maximize the uncanny innate talents of one of the greatest NFL multi-threat talents to ever play the game.

Tebow's 125.6 passer rating was the highest in Broncos postseason history. For the season, Tebow passed for 1729-yards and 12-touchdowns, with 660-yards rushing on 122-attempts for another 6-touchdowns and an outrageous per-carry average. Bringing something team ownership groups covet in their team leaders. Not just talents and skills, but an indomitable will to win.

The guy who's not good enough to play in the NFL. But delivered one of the most entertaining comeback seasons in NFL history. Maybe the single greatest "most-unlikely comeback" ever, to make the playoffs in NFL history. With five 4th-quarter comeback victories and 3- overtime wins.

And against Pittsburgh, a pass to end the game on the first play from scrimmage in overtime to vindicate his unorthodox "force of will" leadership style. And this guy has been out of the NFL?

He beat Pittsburgh in his first try in his first playoff game as an NFL Pro. How many quarterbacks have achieved the equal? Tebow would thrive in the multi-threat "UNIT" offense of the future. Where more than one multi-threat playmaker shares in taking snaps, running for ground gains and passing for playoff wins.

Quarterback prospects of the future should be evaluated by a balanced analysis of their 1) quickness, speed, elusiveness and 2) drive, volition and will to win. It is ludicrous to grade players like Cam Newton, RG III, Tim Tebow and other multi-threat playmakers based on the pocket passer playbook orientation of small NFL mindsets that minimize such talents instead of exploiting them!

8

SAVE THE DAY

There are many ways things can change or go wrong in football. Take a talent like Johnny Manziel. Who may be worthy of his self-titled claim as Johnny Football for how he delivered in college. But who is this guy really? Who is Johnny Football if he's forced to play from a pocket passer playbook? Like happened when Cincinnati held his Shanahan-coached offense scoreless in the playmaker's big rookie start.

For that matter, who is any great player who can't play to their potential when they're recovering from injury or coming off a surgery? I'll tell you who they are. Just another athlete in rehab making a come back...

"Johnny Benchwarmer."

Through my sophomore year in high school I experienced nothing but the best in football. My broken arm the only exception, and I came back even stronger. Scoring so many touchdowns I was written up in the school newspaper and compared to the greatest players in school history.

But I met with great misfortune in Spring Training when I took a hit from a buddy and dislocated my shoulder. Then my doctor discovered it was no typical injury, but a very unusual deformity in the joint he'd never seen. The expectations for my future in football were still on track when I scheduled my summer surgery.

The night before operating on my shoulder, my surgeon visited my hospital room to tell me about the procedure. But when he started explaining how he planned to "fix" things he about scared me to death. First, the injury was caused by a deformity to the ball in my shoulder socket. So the socket was fine, but the ball was half round with one half missing. He said it looked like a half moon and there was no way to really repair it.

The only way to quasi-fix the joint was to basically amputate my arm by cutting everything that held it on, and sewing it back tighter. He assured me it would work, but warned the surgery would be worse than the injury. He was going to cut off my arm basically, he said. Then reattach it. But I would be able to play football again when it healed.

"Here, let me show you…" he said taking a pen from his shirt pocket, clicking it and sitting on the edge of my bed. Then explaining it in detail as he drew rough sketches on my sheet. After he left I called my best friend and said it sounded scary and he was reassuring, but I kept looking at the freehand drawings. Good grief, what a bad idea to draw all that right by my pillow.

It was a sleepless night till the nurse came to wheel me to the operating room early the next morning. When they started my anesthesia I remember someone saying, "Count backwards from 10…" and I started counting, 10, 9, 8…

When I woke up I was nauseated and in excruciating pain. I remember asking for pain medication and having them bring me a shot of morphine. What a great rescue drug for people in severe pain. Except I started vomiting after the shot, though the nurse said it wasn't the morphine, it was the anesthesia making me sick.

They didn't just cut me open and repair one tendon or one ligament or one muscle. I mean, I was HURTING BAD after that surgery and they had me in a wrap of bandage that went around my chest and left shoulder to keep everything perfectly still. The first time they changed the bandaging the nurse said, "Here, hold your arm," and motioned for me to support my arm with my free hand.

All was fine while she was changing it until I barely let my arm drop… O God! I groaned and almost passed out from the intensity of that incredible pain. The nurse barked, "I told you to hold your arm!" I mumbled something back, but that ULTRA-SHARP and DEEP PAIN was something I had never experienced as a young teen.

When the season rolled around my shoulder didn't feel close to recovered, and my surgeon warned me to take it slow. And so it was, I started my first real season of varsity football on the bench, working out in the weight room, working with the trainers under our team doctor's supervision, giving my wounded wing time to heal, and not playing football. I couldn't practice or play the first two games, but then the team doctor cleared me for full contact just before we played the new state champions.

Full Contact! Really, I was wondering? There was just no way. No possible way I was ready for full contact. I didn't think so anyway. It didn't feel like it to me! It hadn't been a full three months since the surgery. How could I be ready for full contact? I felt maybe barely half-recovered. But the show must go on in Texas high school football, and our biggest regular season challenge was coming up so all hands were needed on deck.

The idea of taking a hit on that shoulder made me queasy. But I was cleared for full contact, and in those days you were supposed to play no matter what. If you could breathe and knew your birth date you were good to go, ready to roll.

It was really discouraging because my sophomore highlights should have been for the varsity team, not the JV team. I should have been helping us make the playoffs and advance to the state finals. But Coach refused to play me when I was healthy, despite knowing my talent, instincts and consistent stats.

The team doctor said I should refrain from any contact during practice that same week, and said he'd already told Coach. So I was in shorts and shoulder pads all week leading up to the game, which seemed strange? Why would I be cleared for full contact, then told not to have any contact until the actual day of the game? What? I couldn't help wonder if I was really okay for full contact…

Why could I have no contact before the game? It sounded more like I wasn't ready and they knew it.

The stadium was packed and we started off with a small guy at tailback who had no speed and no running skills. I was trying to steel myself mentally for the first contact in case Coach played me. That first hit… Good Lord! Since I hadn't had any contact up until that night. None, not one hit. Then the backup tailback got hurt and I was abruptly sent into the game. Oh no, was all I could think running on the field. Oh no, here goes! Could I take a hit or not?

Coach called the next play to me, and the quarterback handed me the ball on a dive into the line. I hit the hole and picked up almost 5-yards, feeling the rush and thrill of playing again in that burst of a moment. Then I got held up by several tacklers, just long enough to take a perfect direct hit, directly on my left shoulder that I never saw coming.

Holy God Almighty!

There is no way to describe what the impact of that hit felt like. You talk about seeing stars. It was the most excruciating pain I had ever felt! I fumbled the ball instantly. The pain went through my body like I'd been hit by a truck and struck by lightning at the same time. It made me nauseous and dizzy… O my God! If my shoulder was okay for full-contact, then the rest of me wasn't. It was the most severe pain I ever felt in my life.

I got off the ground with my eyes blurring, and realized they had recovered my fumble. I grabbed a teammate who was helping me up. "They hit my shoulder," I said slurring my words as I grabbed hold of him. He helped me to my feet and held me as we were coming off the field. Approaching the sideline I saw Coach all agitated, coming towards us. "YOU FUMBLED THE BALL…" he screamed at me. "YOU TURNED IT OVER!"

I could still feel the electricity of the pain shock and couldn't even answer. What was I doing trying to play? What was I thinking? But at least I had my first full contact hit behind me.

The game swung back and forth with several lead changes in the second half. A classic battle between two great teams. I got back in the game a couple times, but no plays were called to me. Then, with just over 2-minutes to play, we scored to take the lead and it looked like we were going to beat the reigning state champions.

We kicked off and they took over, ready for one last drive to score the final winning touchdown as time ran out. There was no sense of panic among them. They were a seasoned championship team poised and confident as they picked up 1-first down very quickly. Then another... Advancing the ball way too easily with plenty of time left to score.

Coach was coming undone when all of a sudden he collapsed to the ground. Our coaches ran to his aid as trainers rushed over too. I happened to see it, and thought he had a heart attack. The referee came over and there was a short pause in the game. Then Coach got up and said he was fine. So the game resumed, and the next play they picked up another first down, taking the ball just past midfield around our 45-yard line.

At that, Coach called timeout and huddled with the assistant coaches as we stood by watching and waiting. The game was hanging in the balance and it wasn't looking good for us. Our defense was kaput, done for the night. Running on vapor and fumes, no gas left in the tank. They'd given it everything and had nothing left. We stood watching as the coaches stayed huddled the whole timeout, without talking to any players.

As the ref was running over to restart play, they finally broke the huddle, all stepping back at the same time. Then everything got weird fast, as Coach came rushing quickly, directly over to ME, looking like he was seething mad!

I was wishing I could disappear, since I didn't know what I did to anger him. He got right in my face in front of all my teammates and everybody in the stands.

"I HAVE TO PLAY YOU! AH-h-h..." he screamed with a fading yell.

"I HAVE TO PLAY YOU..." he yelled again, then grit his teeth at me.

Of course, I was stunned. He had to play me? What was he talking about? What did he mean? On defense… At that moment in the game…

We weren't on offense. Why did he have to play me? I didn't even know our defensive sets. I didn't play defense. I was playing tailback on offense. But he was obviously serious. There was a growl-like sound coming out of his throat as he stood snarling without saying anything, and I stood waiting.

What irony… How could you have a more convoluted storyline?

We didn't get to meet this same team for the state championship the year before, partly because Coach wouldn't play me. He wouldn't play me a single play the year before when I was a sophomore. But in the next biggest BIG game since our semifinal loss in Houston… With barely a minute left…

Coach suddenly had to play ME ?

On defense ??

Spitting and spewing, Coach yelled for me to line up deep middle and *"DON'T LET ANYBODY GET PAST YOU!"*

He shoved me to the field… I caught my balance and ran out to line up for the next play. Talk about <u>no warning</u>!

How could anyone in my shoes have seen it coming? As bizarre as could be, the whole thing reminded me of my old fun-coach from 7th grade who told me I was F-R-E-E safety, go out and cover the whole field by myself. And I delivered with back-to-back interceptions to win the game.

Hard to believe… But the same thing was happening again. Only this time in a high school varsity game against the state champs on their field! And my only instructions were to cover the whole field somehow! Figure it out and don't let anybody get past me, on either side of the field!

The math was simple enough.

Despite not liking me, and being jealous of me… There was nobody as fast as I was on our team for Coach to go to. And probably nobody faster on their team. Our coaches knew that. They had seen me play. It appeared as though the coaches had talked Coach into playing me, though he didn't want to. Coach told me that much himself. We had lots of other defensive playmakers on our team besides me. But nobody faster, so it made sense.

The other team was poised to beat us on any long pass play. So, it made perfect sense. Play me as FREE safety because of my speed and playmaking reputation as a last gasp effort to hang on and win. Why not? There was nothing to lose, except the game.

But imagine a head coach running up like that. Yelling in your face when you're not even a defensive player. Letting you know he didn't want to play you. Imagine being called upon by the biggest jerk of all time to go save the day for him. And if you don't cover the entire field by yourself and they score... It's YOUR fault!

YOU are the scapegoat who failed your team. Though your Coach sends you in at no real position, but just deep middle, far right and far left. Cover the entire field by yourself, or else.

When I got where I thought he might have wanted me, their offense broke the huddle and came to the line. No time to think. They were overloaded to my right, with a solo receiver to my left. The quarterback bent down under center and took the snap on a quick count... Game on!

The solo receiver was running a short out route to my left, as the other receivers were running what looked like two streaks and a crossing route underneath to my right. The QB fake-looked strong side, pump-faked, then rolled back to the weak side giving the solo receiver to my left time to break out of his fake route, and turn up the sideline with a blast of speed. Running right past our cornerback who bit on the fake, the receiver was wide open with nobody left to stop him but me, in seconds.

What a thing of beauty, how their championship stars were clicking on all cylinders in that last drive... Then their quarterback drew back and launched his pass high and deep downfield, perfectly on the mark to hit his fleet-footed receiver for the go-ahead touchdown and WIN!

Game almost over...

But I reacted to each part of the play. Running forward first, not giving up left or right. When I saw the solo receiver starting to break past our cornerback, and their QB roll back to the weak side... I committed 100% in an instant burst of quickness then top-speed, sprinting across the field to intersect the receiver as he ran free toward the goal line.

Had I reacted any slower, I wouldn't be writing this right now. But I committed well before the pass was thrown. So I had a chance. A thin chance to stop the play, and I was the only player on our team who could possibly do it. Our cornerback was trailing 5-yards behind, totally out of the play.

The crowd was on their feet. This was the play of the game! Undeniably! A great 4th quarter comeback victory for the reigning champs. And their execution was flawless. On a line to intersect the pass reaching its target, I kept running as fast as I could. Closing on the receiver as the ball came spiraling down from the top of its arch... It was all or nothing. Make or break. In my last steps I gathered my momentum and shot high up in the air.

I jumped first. Then he jumped. Both of us leaping to reach the ball as high as possible. Getting to the same place at the same time. Cradling our arms in a tangled double basket for the ball to land in. His arms in mine, mine in his. The pass was up for grabs. We bumped facemasks at the apex as the ball landed in both of our arms and hands. High, high up in the air... glancing off of each other as we caught the ball together... But I had jumped higher than he did, and I wrestled the ball away from him, pulling it tight up against the numbers on my jersey.

Interception!

Flying out of bounds from the momentum of my leap, I saw the white stripe below and knew I had to stay in bounds for the interception to count. Tilting my body to keep my toes in bounds, I came down in front of the ref and held on when I hit the ground. He blew his whistle.

Turnover!

From the jaws of defeat at the hands of the defending state champions. To the joy of victory in my hands for my team.

Ballgame!

The home crowd was stunned silent. Our bench went ballistic, running over to mob me on the ground before I could get up since it happened on our sideline. They kept piling on till I could hardly breathe. What an incredible interception! What a thrilling play! What a fantastic effort to keep my feet in bounds so they didn't get the ball back for one more try. What a way to redeem myself with Coach!

INCREDIBLE! Coach put me in **to save the game,** and that's what I did.

In 1-play.

The next day one sports writer's front-page coverage described it in those exact words. Using my name and the phrase **"saved the game"** together. What a way to deliver for my team and coaches. My legs were still good! I still had my speed! I still had my heart. I still had my hands! I may not have been a defensive player at the time, but I made the defensive play of the year to win the game for our team, and for Coach.

I got up staggering to get my bearings. Smiling so big, my teammates slapping my shoulder pads and helmet... That was the coolest moment ever. I was vindicated. Coach had been wrong about me. I was a champion! A great playmaker and team leader with a powerful will to do whatever necessary to overcome whatever odds! Making my way to the bench my teammates parted in front of me.

Then I saw Coach and realized he didn't look happy. No, he looked mad. Furious... It didn't make sense. I slowed and came to a stop. Coach rushed up and got in my face as my blood turned cold in my veins. He hunched his shoulders like he was about to hit me. I flinched...

"YOU SHOULDA' KNOCKED IT DOWN !!" he yelled.

"YOU SHOULDA' KNOCKED IT DOWN !!"

Everything drained out of me instantly, is what it felt like. Time stopped in that strange insane moment. Everything went dead inside in the next breath. I don't think I had a pulse. Our stands were going crazy, but I had gone dead to all feeling.

From ecstasy to infamy... Glory to shame... It was a moment that would become a HUGE void in my life for many years... Like I passed through a time warp and entered some level of hell or something. I was aware I was standing in front of Coach in the bright stadium lights. In front of our stands full of wildly cheering fans. But I couldn't really feel anything. Not even my shoulder hurt anymore.

I was trying to take in what Coach was yelling, but I couldn't hear him so I just stood there. His mouth was moving and I could see his amped up aggressive body language. But I think I went into shock maybe. I don't know what that feels like. But everything seemed so surreal. Maybe that's what shock feels like.

Someone could have stabbed me in the heart and I wouldn't have known it.

That play was a major setback to my recovery from shoulder surgery, but I never said anything afterwards. Coach treated injured players worse than anybody else, so I wasn't going to make things worse for myself on purpose.

The rest of my junior season was one injury after another, as I kept playing hurt and getting hurt. The trainers had warned me: Play hurt, get hurt. I proved their theory true. Ending up with both ankles sprained and a slew of other injuries. A shell of myself as a player that season after the game in Austin... A step slower, three steps late, with tape and bandages holding me together.

I kept getting more injuries playing hurt, instead of healing first. I hurt my left ankle at the end of practice mid-season, after hurting the other one the day before. Hobbling on two bad ankles, I went from the field to the trainers who gave me several different treatments to try and salvage me for more football.

Coming out when they let me go, I saw all my teammates had left as I walked to the cage to dress and go home. But there was a commotion in the coach's office and I glanced up to see it was Coach... Oh sh- - !!

He almost jumped out of his chair to bolt out of the office and come running over... By the time he reached the door to the cage, I was turning to sit where I hung my uniform. Coach rushed up in a frantic madness...

"You're HURT! You're ALWAYS HURT! Because YOU'RE AFRAID of getting HURT!" He was so out of control I didn't dare move. "You're ALWAYS getting HURT," he kept shouting. I saw the trainer step out behind him at the training room door, to see what was going on.

"NOW, LOOK AT YOU," Coach yelled. Violating and humiliating me for nothing... I could only sit still and watch. I knew not to move. When he finished crushing my spirit, the trainer stepped back quickly into the training room right as Coach turned, walked out of the cage and went back to his office.

I never felt emptier in my life than that moment. Never felt more like giving up.

I had almost no feeling or physical sensation, after yet another abusive tirade by Coach, who always delivered the same body language with the same threatening, intimidating ANGST to the HILT.

I remember wondering why none of the other coaches did anything to stop him from destroying me like that. How do you justify treating a great young athlete so abusively over an injury? How do you justify treating anybody like that? Just because I was injured and having to play hurt... But none of the assistant coaches did a thing to challenge him, and Coach got away with doing it again.

Leaving me dead inside and wanting to quit. Why was I playing for this guy?

By our last game, I was a mess of bruises, cuts, tape and blood. But I was playing football in Texas. Trailing at halftime, things were not okay in our locker under the stands. We would advance to the playoffs with a win, or miss the playoffs with a loss. All of us were sitting with helmets off, listening to Coach rant and rave at us. When he turned to me and stopped talking.

Oh sh- - Not again!

He stepped over slowly. I didn't flinch this time. I started clinching my teeth, as whatever Coach had been killing inside me started to *COME BACK TO LIFE!* My lips were closed, but I was gritting my teeth. Coach stuck his clipboard in my face...

"And YOU... ALL YOU WANT TO DO IS PROTECT YOUR BODY! That's all you want! To PROTECT YOUR BODY!"

In a flash of fury I suddenly didn't care anymore. All I wanted to do was hurt Coach as bad as I could. I wanted to hit him in the mouth and break his face. I wanted to knock him out cold.

He was NOT going to disrespect me in front of my teammates AGAIN! He was NOT going to humiliate me AGAIN! I wasn't afraid of him anymore. I had been sacrificing my body all season for my team. What he said wasn't true. I was playing with all my heart and all my guts for him. I just wasn't healthy.

Watching his clipboard get close to my face, I started gripping my facemask getting ready to take my helmet back, so I could... He stepped away from me abruptly.

Maybe he saw the hate in my eyes, I don't know. But I felt the HATE in my heart and I felt the reflex to HIT him with my helmet. But he stepped back from me, and it was too late.

Years later Coach made front-page news when he injured his starting quarterback with a clipboard. In some rant at his players the maniac let fly his clipboard and it slashed his young star QB across the face. Surprise, surprise... I couldn't help wonder if it was the same clipboard he shook at me the night I almost tried to kill him with my helmet.

I recovered over the next several months, and after a superlative track season of just enjoying being a young athlete again. I got the surprise of my life when Coach called me in for a talk before Spring Training. I was wary and untrusting, of course. But Coach was approaching me respectfully for a change.

I settled in a chair across from him and listened as he explained how he'd been thinking, and had decided, he wanted me to start taking snaps at quarterback.

I was beyond shocked.

I could hardly believe my ears. I did not like the man, and did not trust him. But Coach was treating me okay for a change. Then he had me start taking snaps at QB in practice. I was getting to return to my "multi-threat" running quarterback-of-the-future position. The position I played as good as anybody I've ever seen play football: Scatback Quarterback!

Some new energy started welling up in me, almost. Getting to play freestyle running quarterback again! Almost I say, because a different fate was lurking just around the corner for me.

Who knows why it happened to me? I guess my football future just wasn't meant to be. Because right when it looked like I might be returning to my real position of running quarterback, I tore the ACL in my right knee in a crazy downpour during the Spring Game. The floodgates of heaven opened and the sky turned black. It was like playing in a hurricane and a nightmare at the same time. I slipped in the mud. Someone fell on my extended leg. My knee bent the wrong direction.

Next thing I knew, I was scheduling my second consecutive summer surgery.

No, it didn't seem possible. No, it wasn't fair. Not another major injury! Not another major surgery! It was so discouraging. So wrong... No.

No, was all I could think.

No. No. No.

But, yes… Just like that, my immediate football future was over.

Multi-Threat Highlights & History

Johnny Manziel

Youth

Johnny Manziel was born in Tyler, Texas to Michelle and Paul Manziel on December 6, 1992. He grew up playing a variety of sports including basketball, baseball, golf and football. It was at Tivy High School in Kerrville, Texas, where Johnny shortlisted baseball and football as the two sports he would play. However, football was where his greatest talents lied.

High School

Under the tutelage of Mark Smith at the Tivy High School, Manziel played football all four years there and began with the freshman team in his first year. Such were his displays that by the end of his first season, he had played with the varsity team as a receiver. Then came the sophomore year where he was primarily deployed as a receiver again but then started the fourth game at quarterback.

He shared that position for the remainder of the campaign and finished with 1,164 yards passing, 806 rushing and 408 receiving for a combined number of 28 touchdowns. Manziel's junior year was the first time he actually started as a starting quarterback. In that season, he ended with 2,903 passing yards, 1,544 rushing yards, 152 receiving yards and 55 touchdowns. Such performances led him to be voted All-San Antonio Area Offensive Player of the Year as well as the District 27-4A MVP.

In his senior season, Johnny Manziel compiled 228-of-347 (65.7 %) passing for 3,609 yards with 45 TDs and 5 INTs. He also had 170 carries for 1,674 yards and 30 TDs. He had 1 TD reception and returned a kickoff for a touchdown for a combined number of 77 TDs.

In the same year, he was honored as District 28-4A MVP, Class 4A First Team All-State (AP), San Antonio Express News Offensive Player of the Year (an award he landed second year in a row), the Associated Press Sports Editors Texas Player of the Tear, Sub-5A First Team All-Area (SA Express News), No. 1 QB in Texas by Dave Campbell's Texas Football, DCTF Top 300, PrepStar All-Region and Super-Prep All-Region.

With a glut of awards for his performances, Manziel entered his third season with a lot of confidence. By the end of his three years as a starting quarterback, Manziel had completed 520 of 819 passes (boasting a percentage of 63.5), for 7,626 yards and 76 touchdowns, rushed 531 times for 4,045 yards and 77 touchdowns and caught 30 passes for 582 yards and another five touchdowns.

He was the only quarterback in America who was named as a Parade All-American his senior year and was also named The National High School Coaches Association (NHSCA) Senior Athlete of the Year in Football.

Consistently commanding performances in school showed Johnny Manziel was the talent for the future, which is why he became one of the most sought after players out of high school. Many college programs vied for his signature. In addition to Texas A&M, Manziel received offers from Baylor, Colorado State, Iowa State, Louisiana Tech, Oregon, Rice, Stanford, Tulsa and Wyoming. Many thought Manziel would end up signing for Texas Longhorns whom he supported as a kid.

However, the University of Texas did not recruit him and there were rumors that the coach Mack Brown wanted him only as a defensive back. After committing to play for Oregon, the he changed his mind and signed with the Aggies. The greatest influence behind this change of heart was quarterback coach Tom Rossley.

College

Johnny Manziel accepted the athletic scholarship to attend Texas A&M University where he played for the Aggies from 2011 to 2013.

For the 2011 season, Manziel was redshirted and did not play in any games. The 2012 season however, was an entirely different story. After Ryan Tannehill left to play in the NFL, it left the coaching staff at Texas A&M with decisions to make for their quarterback position.

During the Spring and Fall practices, Manziel performed very well and deservedly won the starting job over Jameill Showers and Matt Joeckel before the season began. The youngster was in line to make his debut against Louisiana Tech in Shreveport, Louisiana. However, the game was postponed due to Hurricane Isaac hitting the coast a couple of days before.

Manziel made his debut in the game against the Florida Gators at the Kyle Field. After beginning the season without any real fireworks, Manziel came to life in the game against Arkansas. During one play, he broke Archie Manning's 43-year-old total offense record. Manziel had 557 yards of total offense, which was better than Manning's record of 540. That got a lot of attention and two games later, Manziel surpassed his own total offense record against #24 Louisiana Tech by racking up 576 yards of total offense.

Johnny Manziel became the first player in the history of the SEC to have two 500 plus total offense games in one season. Following Texas A&M's blowout of Auburn in game eight, during which Manziel accounted for 3 passing and 2 rushing touchdowns through the first half plus one series in the second, the young quarterback began showing up in national Heisman Watch lists.

It was his performance in Texas A&M's 29-24 upset win over #1 Alabama in Tuscaloosa that propelled Manziel onto the national scene. In that game, he accounted for 345 of A&M's 418 yards of offense, including two passing touchdowns.

In the coming days, Manziel's stock rose to new heights and he became the frontrunner for the Heisman Trophy in most national watch lists and polls due to his performances combined with other Heisman frontrunners faltering when it mattered the most.

In late November, during the game against the Missouri Tigers in front of a home crowd, Manziel left the game with a knee injury in the first quarter. However, he returned to the field for the next series of downs with a knee brace and remarkably, finished the game with 439 yards of total offense, including 3 passing and 2 rushing touchdowns. During the same game, Manziel also broke the single season record for offensive production in the SEC with a whopping 4600 yards – a record that was held by Cam Newton and Tim Tebow.

He also became the first ever freshman and only the fifth player in the history of NCAA to pass for 3000 and rush for 1000 yards in a single season. He reached that mark two games earlier than any other player.

Following his excellent season, Johnny Manziel also won the SEC Freshman of the Year Award and College Football Performance National Freshman of the Year Award. Manziel won the Davey O'Brien Award early in December and to cap off an amazing season, won the Heisman Trophy and became the first freshman to win either award.

Texas A&M started the 2013 campaign with a No. 6 ranking in the Coaches Poll. Prior to the season, a few journalists predicted Johnny to suffer from a sophomore slump, while others suggested the budding quarterback would continue having success.

In the game against No. 1 Alabama, Manziel threw for a school record of 464 yards and five touchdowns. His primary target for that game was Mike Evans, who compiled seven receptions for a school record of 279 yards. In the 51-41 win over Mississippi State, Manziel tied his career high five touchdowns while throwing for 446 yards.

In 2012 Johnny Manziel made 434 pass attempts out of which 295 were completed. His completion percentage was 68.0. He gained 3,706 passing yards, passed for 26 TDs and boasted a passer rating of 155.3. He also rushed for 1,410 yards and 21 touchdowns.

The 2013 season saw further improvement in Manziel's passing as he completed 300 of 429 passes and boasted a completion percentage of 69.9. His passing yards improved as well. He threw for 4,114 yards and 37 touchdowns and boasted a passer rating of 172.9 while rushing for 759 yards and 9 touchdowns.

Overall, his two years at Texas A&M saw Manziel complete 595 out of 863 passes and a pass completion percentage of 68.9. He threw for 7,820 yards, 63 touchdowns, boasting an average passer rating of 164.1 while rushing for another 2,169 yards and 30 TDs.

NFL career

On January 8, 2014, Manziel announced he would be forgoing his junior season in order to enter the 2014 NFL Draft. He was projected to be a first round pick and as of January 15, 2014, his draft stock was reported to be rising by a consensus of experts who had him pegged as a top-5 pick. On March 27, 2014, Manziel chose to throw during Texas A&M's Pro Day instead of during the NFL Combine.

During his pro day, he completed 64 of 66 passes to six different receivers, in a performance that drew a lot of acclaim from many sports journalists.

On May 8, 2014, Manziel was selected by the Cleveland Browns as the 22nd pick of the first round of the 2014 NFL Draft. .

A lot of credit for Texas A&M's offensive success in Manziel's two seasons goes down to his performances. Manziel is as quick as any elite footballer and like Michael Vick can escape from the pocket to keep plays alive. He has the ability to evade rushers and attack either from the open field as a runner or by finding open receivers downfield.

Although he had the luxury of three future NFL starters as his offensive tackles in Luke Joeckel, Jake Matthews and Cedric Ogbuehi, Manziel has been very consistent in being able to make one or more rushers miss in their pursuit and forcing teams to have five or six defenders in the box against him, this allowing for the potential of more one-on-one matchups.

Today's NFL is becoming more open to quarterback prospects such as Manziel. If used correctly and wisely, Manziel's unique skills could translate from college fervor to NFL wins.

The offense needs to be tailored initially to his threat as a runner, forcing defenses to contain and neutralize him. Manziel is a unique talent whose creativity and improvisation as a quarterback could help him achieve great success.

Pros

Manziel was drafted by the Cleveland Browns and began his career with the Browns learning the system as the team's second-string quarterback. Getting limited minutes as a rookie, Manziel's future potential in the NFL is yet to be seen, but expectations suggest he could become a force if and when he is allowed to shine.

Like any other great multi-threat quarterback prospects today, it will never happen as long as he is forced to play out of a scripted pocket passer playbook. If and when Manziel gets an opportunity to play to his strengths, from a new and revised playbook of the future... Will he have matured enough to take his NFL opportunity serious enough to make anything of it?

Showing no convincing interest in improving his image of professionalism, and preferring to distance himself from his teammates continuing his college-like freewheeling lifestyle. Manziel's success may depend most on whether he grows up enough before blacklisting himself around the league by his own actions.

9

COME WHAT MAY

My ACL was torn and couldn't be fixed, so my doc operated but did not repair the torn ligament. He cleaned out the mess of torn cartilage and that's all they could do before technology got to where athletes can have a torn ACL replaced.

Back in the day they would say build up the muscles around your knee. I'm serious. That was it. What else could you do? Your only option was to get your leg muscles stronger. And that was supposed to hold your knee in place better. Pseudo-science is what it was. But honestly, even with the quarterback position open, I had lost my passion to play football. Coach had broken my will to play the game I loved.

I did not want to play for him.

He had me second-guessing everything I did, telling me I was wrong to save the game with my interception in Austin. Playing hurt and enduring all the abuse took the enjoyment out of the game. Blowing out my knee sealed the deal. When I officially quit the team it was written up in the Sports section of the local paper. My last hurrah came with the writer saying my team had "lost a lot" in losing me. But in reality, Coach lost me long before the injury.

That's why I have a special place in my heart for athletes who get mismatched with the wrong coaches or playbooks. Like RG-III and Shanahan... Vince Young and Jeff Fischer.

Call whichever party guilty you want. When a coach FAILS at helping a great athlete transition… No matter what anybody says, the coach bears 50% of the responsibility. **Or more…** Great talents come with great wills to do great things. For a coach to fail at helping the talent do greater things boggles my mind, except I lived to see it done to me. So, I get it.

My question is, "Why?"

The coach had what the other coaches wanted. The great athlete! With the great drive and talent, and will force to deliver! There is always a way to coach and direct a great athlete for better or worse. To draw out his best takes the right coaching for the individual player. When a coach gets nothing from star potential, and does more to hold it back than launch it. That says more about the coach than the player in my book.

There is no doubt Vince Young made mistakes in his career. And no doubt another coach could have done a better job than Fischer. Same for Shanahan and RG-III. When a coach loses a star I hate it. I had it happen to me. I know firsthand, as the wasted talent.

It is the coach's job to get it done. When he is provided the greatest athlete with the greatest talent, heart, drive and will. Getting nothing out of that arrangement is NOT acceptable. If another coach could do a better job, the coach who failed bears the responsibility.

NOT THE ATHLETE !!

What Shanahan did with Elway and Terrell Davis was a beautiful thing. I was living in Colorado, I can speak to that experience personally. How Shanahan's coaching declined after he lost Elway and Davis was hard to watch. I remember knowing all was lost when he called a screen pass on 3rd and two in the red zone, from around the 15-yard line. No, it didn't work! They lost yardage, of course. When Washington hired the fired coach the handwriting was on the wall.

Coaches don't live forever, and neither do their game plans. RG-III will blossom more the more he gets an offensive coach to custom-design a playbook around his skills. Same for all other great multi-threat quarterbacks in the NFL. They're desperate for a playbook with new innovative plays that aren't so predictable.

If anything is lacking in NFL football today, it is a decent playbook for the multi-threat offensive talents in the league. I feel sorry for the incredible multi-threat quarterbacks of the future playing today. The typical playbook just isn't getting it done. Not well enough to help these multitalented athletes prove me right, for saying they will take over NFL offenses in the future. Thankfully, some offensive coordinators are playing with the variables and creating new read-option plays. Which is why I'm watching the NFL again.

My senior year of high school I didn't go to a single football game. I turned my attention to healing. More coaches need to insist on this approach as team policy. Let the athlete HEAL first. And if there was ever a good example of how injured athletes should be handled, it's Gregg Popovich of the NBA San Antonio Spurs.

Popovich has a simple way of handling a recovering athlete's return. First, the athlete must heal. What a novel idea… Whether Pop is beardless or in whiskers, that's how it is for every injured player of the multi-champion San Antonio Spurs. The player must heal first, then get into "practice" condition next.

No exceptions. No shortcuts.

They must get into "GAME" condition before the healed athlete is deemed ready to play "limited" minutes. If you were ever an injured athlete like me, this is a very logical and appropriate way to bring an injured player back to playing again.

I skipped track season my senior year. Out of school by noon, I would run by the house for lunch then head to my job at a local sporting goods store till 9:00 pm every night. Didn't go to my graduation, but was voted Most Talented by my peers despite not participating in extracurricular activities or the talent show. It was an honor to the inglorious ending of a young talent's place in Texas football lore. I really appreciated my classmates for recognizing me like that.

The brutal way my football career ended left a lot of wounds to heal. Of course, I hated it. But things don't always work like they should in life, do they? And I had new highlights to experience in my senior year. Like getting promoted to manager at the sporting goods store and buying a hunting rifle with my employee discount for Christmas.

I'd lost my passion to play the way I played. Nothing mattered to me anymore. I had always felt it was my responsibility to win the game for my team. But after Coach got finished with me that was gone. And the excitement did not return until I got to coach my son's youth-league football team years later.

When... Without the negativity from the top, it was FUN again!

Imagine that. O yea! Getting to coach the way I thought kids and teenagers should be coached was the ultimate vindication. In a spirited, uplifting, encouraging way where my team enjoyed playing the game while learning how to be their best. Yes, and amen!

That's how simple it is folks. What else could be better than helping players enjoy being their best, within the concept of team play? Not to mention, I got to experiment with my multi-threat "QB Unit" ideas like I had played as a kid. Oh yea! It's a kid's game first, right? And I did it all with a distinct, but simple advantage. A smile on my face! Yep, my teams had FUN playing football. Like how it was FUN when I played. The FUN of the game wasn't missing... It was everything we did.

Unconventional... Outside the box... Three running QB's leading the way.

Three of our most talented, quickest and fastest multi-threat playmakers sharing responsibility as our co-leaders. And they were just kids! How did three kids make it look so easy? Maybe it really wasn't that hard. Maybe it was simple. Maybe depending on each other helped them work together better. All three in the game at the same time... One lined up as a receiver, the other two split behind center 4-yards deep and 4-yards apart as running passers.

Playing together. Switching positions all game long. There was no way to know what we would do next, when we didn't always know ourselves. Our plays could morph into new things that worked. Out of broken plays that didn't work. Like how I played when I was a kid. We always had more options because we could always run for it. And the defense never knew which of The Three might pass or pitch or run.

We were unpredictable and that changed the game in our favor. It may sound confusing to a reader, but it wasn't confusing to us. We knew what we were doing. Basing our plays in simple sets with multiple options was the key. It was very simple for our players to learn the basic parameters.

The unpredictability that was confusing to the defense, was not confusing to us. The concept was empowering. And it was freeing to be empowered. That made it easy. The Three had to play together for it to work. Had to make the catch, make the throw, make the block for each other. And they did, in a win-win approach that led us to a shot at back-to-back championships.

The over-emphasis of depending on a single prima donna, one-dimensional drop back passer wasn't there. Our starting quarterback was never knocked out of a single game all season. Why? Because we didn't have a starting quarterback. We had three!

But there was more to the concept. I wanted to increase the odds of success from past models. Think about it. What are the simplest most evident things a new strategy could do to give an offense the advantage every time? If YOU were the offensive coordinator of an NFL franchise? What would be the most obvious things YOUR offense might want to do?

Here's what I came up with for my kids:

1. Gain positive yards every play
2. Rarely lose yards any play
3. Rarely lose yards to penalties
4. Extend QB Time to Pass
5. Eliminate QB sacks

6. Consistently pick up 1st downs
7. Consistently convert 4th downs
8. Be unpredictable

The smarter offenses of the future *will come up with ways* to do these things.

#1...

Positive yards every play...

What we did was emphasize NOT GOING BACKWARDS. The ball can move faster than your feet. Ask passing basketball teams about this reality... By not going backwards first, you become more of The Aggressor.

We created a template of moving pocket and option models we could run or throw from. Models we made simple for us, but confusing for the defense. From which we could run all kinds of plays, including Misdirection, Bait and Switch and Read Option plays.

Don't retreat. Advance! That was the premise. Always be threatening advance on all fronts at all times. If the defense reacts to stop one of our runner-quarterback "Unit" playmakers, fine... He will pass it over their heads or run it right by them. Many of our plays looked like part sweep and part rollout with drifting pockets we could run or pass from.

Depending on the run/pass option of the particular play, we would execute the plays at different paces. But most of our plays were run-first, read option pass plays. Allowing our QB Unit playmakers to adjust on the fly, together as one.

Good scatback instincts give a running-passer a big advantage. Everything is a ploy when anything can happen, and everything can change. Is he going to run? Is he going to pass? Is he going to start running- then pitch the ball to a teammate who runs or passes?

Who knows...

An offense that is not on the retreat. What a novel idea. Never on the retreat. All 11-guys more involved in every play. Target trying to pick up 3- or 4-yards running or passing, with the deep pass option in the same play. Go on the attack for heaven's sake! Put the defense on their heels. Line up imbalanced or balanced, then switch and snap the ball quickly. Do unconventional things that are routine for your team, but unpredictable for defenses.

Receivers are in the picture, trying to break free on routes that look like the receiver is going out to block every play. Is it a block? Is it a pass route?

Who knows…

In most instances, it is both as the play is unfolding. The defender is kept wondering. Should they try to get around the blocker to stop the run, or cover the receiver to stop the pass? Or twist their ankle trying to do both at once?

Read option run-or-pass plays allow the Unit QB's to react to what the defenders do. The runner can throw. The passer can run. His Unit QB mates can present one look in the first split second or two of a play. Then lateral the ball to another Scatback QB playmaker and flip the whole play on its head.

#4 –

Extending the Time to Pass while allowing the Scatback QB the option of using his quickness to dash a few yards if the field opens up, rather than risking a bad throw or dropped pass. Moving in a drifting pocket and improvising outside the pocket to buy time to pass, or let the field open for a quick-dash run.

It is very confusing for defenders when plays consistently have the ability to morph into something completely different on the fly.

#2 & #5 –

To rarely lose yards and eliminate sacks, just remember what my dad told me: "Get back to the line of scrimmage no matter what." Simple instructions are easier to follow. Don't let the defenders tackle you behind the line of scrimmage. Very simple. Get back to the line so there's no deficit the next play. It will help the whole team if you never get sacked, so don't.

When this is stressed repeatedly, players will buy in and develop an attitude about it. They know, if things start breaking down THEY MUST FIND A WAY to get back to the line of scrimmage without losing yardage. I did it all the time. This often led to crazy rushing gains. How? Because it surprised everybody! It was so urgent and immediate it would catch the defenders off balance, and a narrow seam would open up sometimes. Depending on how ultra-quick the reaction was to avoid getting sacked. Imagine taking a snap and looking for receivers downfield... You're supposed to pass, but everything goes wrong, there's no way out. What do you do?

By that time, I would be diving for the last yard to get back to the line of scrimmage if I was under pressure. Rarely having sacks or losing yards on running plays would be a huge advantage for any offense in any game, at any level. Incorporating this concept by TRYING to accomplish it makes the difference. It's mandated. No matter what play it is, or what happens during the play, every player knows losing yardage is unacceptable.

How this works is... The players are trained to develop their instincts so they react bullet fast to imminent sacks or tackles behind the line of scrimmage. You tell them in plain English to make sure they react like this. Tell them to abort the play and dive if they have to, to get back to the line of scrimmage. React, not only faster than the defense is expecting, but with MORE INTENT and force-of-will to actually get back to the line of scrimmage or break the play into something new.

Any time they don't achieve this goal and lose a yard or two, is an example to teach from. Explain how you don't want them waiting that long next time. They need to develop a SIXTH SENSE so they ALWAYS manage to get back to the line and NEVER get sacked. This helps them do just that. They consciously develop an innate sense for it...

To avoid losing yards to penalties. Stress the concept by using a whistle in practices. I would over-use the whistle randomly, to the point I was unfair to the players sometimes. Calling the slightest hint of movement before the snap. I would also quietly instruct the defenders to jump into the neutral zone to make offensive linemen flinch. Then blow the whistle and call a motion violation on the offensive lineman for nothing. When they complained, I said it's unfair. Too bad. Then I would assess the penalty and have them start over.

They got infuriated at me for this and I would agree. "You're right it's not fair," I'd say. "Okay, line up…"

I would use these moments to instill in their minds that things aren't going to be fair in games 100% of the time. Get over it. Don't bellyache about it. Don't show any negative body language about it. EVER. The players were trained to overcome all odds in this way. I would say, "So what?" And…"Get over it," until they just stopped saying it wasn't fair and never flinched.

We also simplified the snap count. There are so many ways to describe how a snap count can be simplified, I won't waste time talking about it. Any offensive coordinator could come up with ways to simplify the snap count so there are fewer motion and offside penalties. I stressed that there was nothing to do until the ball was snapped. I would rather everybody start a fraction late, than a fraction early.

#6 –

Improving the team's percentage of picking up first downs on 1st, 2nd and 3rd downs is a simple concept. Too logical to dispute. But how do you do it? Well, not losing yards to sacks and penalties is a good way to start. Having plays that are attacking, not retreating is good idea. Make it significant to your players that you are trying to be one of the top teams at picking up first downs, especially on third down.

Going for it on 4th down should "not" be something you call a timeout for just to decide if you should do it. Make up your mind before the season, what conditions you want to go for it on 4th down more often. Get good at picking up first downs on 4th down by teaching it, training for it, imparting the belief and faith in the idea and doing it in practices and scrimmages in simulated conditions.

A great way to stress any of these ideas?

Simulate game conditions by staging them in practice. Line the team up and tell them the simulated condition. Tell them how you want them to think in such situations in a game. Run the play for the simulated down and game condition you're teaching them to be familiar with. Explain the consequences of the play if it fails. Then run it again in practice like this, over and over again. Players become accustom to a new mindset of getting the job done. When the situation arises in games, their mindset immediately goes into "get it done" mode and it's not as daunting. They've done it before, felt it before, thought it before.

They've been in that game situation many times in practice. Nothing new. Simulating game conditions is essential to unlocking the freedom of will force in athletes to play with their greatest confidence in games by instinct, not just thinking. Having to depend on thinking-things-through before acting in a game won't work. Players have to develop an ability to STAY IN THE MOMENT. Anticipating and reacting more than pondering things mentally.

Finally, #8 –

Never do anything like the traditional drop back pocket passer model, where every defender in the galaxy knows exactly, precisely where you're going to drop back. A great idea if you want to be unpredictable. Like I said, I put two guys back for every snap, and had the snap go back-right or back-left of center every play. Another thing I didn't mention... We did not always snap the ball to the player calling the snap count.

Half the time the ball was snapped to the guy calling the count. Half the time it went to the other Unit QB who did not call the count. We had a lot of bait and switch plays, making it look like we were doing something we weren't really doing. The Unit QB playmakers who were back for the snap would routinely act like they each got the snap. For the first instant of the play. In other words, I'm talking about doing an array of little things to create doubt and/or hesitation in the defenders' minds.

That's how you can be more unpredictable. Just do it! Like the sports product slogan. "Just do it!" For heaven's sake, why not? What would you rather do, be predictable? Too many offensive plays are too PREDICTABLE. Do something about it. That's a better idea than doing nothing.

I think we're close to seeing the Unit QB role develop in the NFL, where you have players like Michael Vick and Geno Smith in the game at the same time. Create a new playbook, of course. Then set the playmakers free. Let these guys go! Let them run more when they can pick up 3- to 4-yards and slide w/out taking a hit. Give them the green light! Plan it ahead of time intentionally.

It's a whole new game when the defense can't depend on knowing in advance most of what you're going to do, as soon as you start doing it, like they can with traditional drop-back passers

Football Injury-Reality Check

Football is a rough sport, and despite the helmets, pads, braces, and supports, regular injuries are a common part of the game. The size of the players, the speed of play and the physical nature of the game makes injuries inevitable in the NFL.

As many as 1.5 million young men participate in American football in the United States. An estimated 1.2 million football-related injuries are sustained annually. Since the 1970s epidemiological studies have shown that the risk of injury is higher in older athletes and lower in teams with more experienced coaches and more assistant coaches. 51% of injuries occurred at training; contact sessions were 4.7 times more likely to produce injuries than controlled sessions.

Wearing shorter cleats and preseason conditioning reduced injury rates. Overall, lower extremity injuries accounted for 50% of all injuries (with knee injuries accounting for up to 36%). Upper extremity injuries accounted for 30%. In general, sprains and strains account for 40% of injuries, contusions 25%, fractures 10%, concussions 5% and dislocations 15%.

Cervical spine injuries have the potential to be catastrophic, but they declined dramatically in the decade 1975 to 1984, due to the impact of rule changes modifying tackling and blocking techniques and improved fitness, equipment and coaching. Appropriate diagnostic evaluation of cervical injuries is mandatory.

The evidence supporting prophylactic knee bracing is not compelling and does not mandate compulsory or routine use. Return to play criteria include: full range of motion; normal strength; normal neurological evaluation; no joint swelling or instability; ability to run and sustain contact without pain; no intake of pain medication; player education about preventive measures and future risks.

These criteria should be strictly observed. In addition to ankle and knee rehabilitation, lumbar spine injuries present a challenge for the physician.

Repetitive flexion, extension and torsional stresses predispose the lumbar spine to injury. Rehabilitation consists of pain control and training.

The training phase aims to eliminate repetitive injuries by minimizing stress at the intervertebral joint. Football is a high-risk sport. Coaches, players, trainers and physicians must all become aware of the proper means to prevent injuries.

NFL Injuries

The data came from a survey conducted at statcrunch.com in 2013 regarding the widely controversial topic of NFL football injuries. There has been an overwhelming focus on player safety in the last 5 years but there are still too many injuries occurring. This data set shows the volume of injuries as well as the type of injuries that occurred during the 2011 NFL season. The data set consists of an accumulation of all the injuries that occurred for all 32 NFL teams in the 2011 NFL season. They chose this topic due to my overall passion for the game of football and interest in neuroscience. They hope to one day get my food in the door in the multi-billion dollar business of the NFL.

To examine this question, they constructed a bar plot to see what the most common injuries in the 2011 NFL season were. Although concussions have played a large role in the emphasis for new player safety, it is knee injuries that seem to be the most common. These results surprised me because all you hear about are the prevention of head injuries while the top 3 injury categories are below the hip. In other words, it appears that the most common injuries to occur to NFL football players are to their lower bodies. Thus, I believe that there should be more of an emphasis on making gains to protect NFL players from lower body injuries.

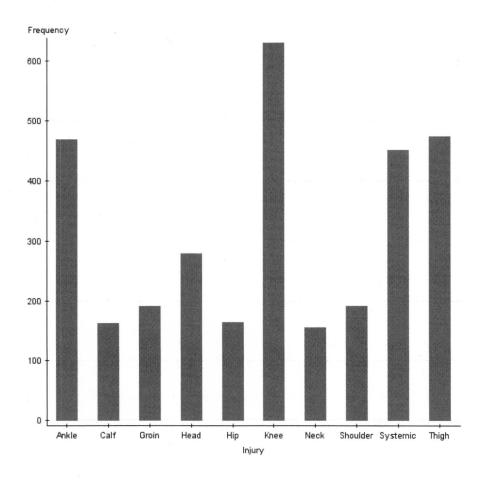

The following is a partial list of some of the injuries we see and treat every day this time of year, related to football:

Knee injuries

The knee is made up of many important structures, any of which can be injured. The most common knee injuries include fractures around the knee, dislocation, and sprains and tears of soft tissues, like ligaments. In many cases, injuries involve more than one structure in the knee.

Pain and swelling are the most common signs of knee injury. In addition, your knee may catch or lock up. Many knee injuries cause instability — the feeling that your knee is giving way.

Fractures

The most common bone broken around the knee is the patella. The ends of the femur and tibia where they meet to form the knee joint can also be fractured. Many fractures around the knee are caused by high-energy trauma, such as falls from significant heights during the match.

Anterior Cruciate Ligament (ACL) Injuries

The anterior cruciate ligament is often injured during sports activities. Athletes who participate in high demand sports like soccer, football, and basketball are more likely to injure their anterior cruciate ligaments. Changing direction rapidly or landing from a jump incorrectly can tear the ACL. About half of all injuries to the anterior cruciate ligament occur along with damage to other structures in the knee, such as articular cartilage, meniscus, or other ligaments.

Posterior Cruciate Ligament Injuries

The posterior cruciate ligament is often injured from a blow to the front of the knee while the knee is bent. This often occurs in motor vehicle crashes and sports-related contact. Posterior cruciate ligament tears tend to be partial tears with the potential to heal on their own.

Collateral Ligament Injuries

Injuries to the collateral ligaments are usually caused by a force that pushes the knee sideways. These are often contact injuries. Injuries to the MCL are usually caused by a direct blow to the outside of the knee, and are often sports-related. Blows to the inside of the knee that push the knee outwards may injure the lateral collateral ligament. Lateral collateral ligament tears occur less frequently than other knee injuries.

Meniscal Tears

Sudden meniscal tears often happen during sports. Tears in the meniscus can occur when twisting, cutting, pivoting, or being tackled. Meniscal tears may also occur as a result of arthritis or aging. Just an awkward twist when getting up from a chair may be enough to cause a tear, if the menisci have weakened with age.

Tendon Tears

The quadriceps and patellar tendons can be stretched and torn. Although anyone can injure these tendons, tears are more common among middle-aged people who play running or jumping sports. Falls, direct force to the front of the knee, and landing awkwardly from a jump are common causes of knee tendon injuries.

Ankle sprains

The damage of soft tissue and ligaments surrounding the ankle is what causes a sprained ankle. The position of the bones around the ankle makes it very susceptible to inversion injury where the ankle becomes twisted inwards.

Inversion injury is also possible where the ankle becomes twisted outwards. Due to excessive twisting, lateral ligaments outside the ankle are over-stretched or damaged. Sprained ankles are common among footballers.

Ankle sprains are graded 1-3, based on severity. The less severe sprains are often easily managed and athletes can return to play within several days to weeks. Football players can also sustain "high ankle sprains," these are more severe and require casting for a short period of time.

Shoulder injuries

There are two common types of shoulder injuries sustained in football:

Shoulder dislocation

Shoulder dislocation occurs when a player's arm is forced outwards and upwards by a tackle or heavy landing and the shoulder joint pops out.

AC separation

An AC separation is also known as a "separated shoulder". This is a tear of the ligaments between the clavicle and acromion bone, which causes the clavicle (collar bone) to stick up. Most of these are treated without surgery, although rehabilitation is often required before returning to play.

Back injuries

Thankfully, these are mostly just sprains, which often respond nicely to bracing and rehabilitation exercise. More severe impacts can cause herniated discs, or even fractures. It is a well-known fact that football players, especially linemen who have had a long career, go on to get arthritis in their backs due to the stress placed on them during their career.

Head injuries

A traumatic brain injury (TBI) is defined as a blow or jolt to the head or a penetrating head injury that disrupts the normal function of the brain. TBI can result when the head suddenly and violently hits an object, or when an object pierces the skull and enters brain tissue. Symptoms of a TBI can be mild, moderate, or severe, depending on the extent of damage to the brain. Mild cases may result in a brief change in mental state or consciousness, while severe cases may result in extended periods of unconsciousness, coma, or even death.

Concussions

Cerebral concussions are considered diffuse brain injuries and can be defined as traumatically induced alterations of mental status. A concussion results from shaking the brain within the skull and, if severe can cause shearing injuries to nerve fibers and neurons.

Grading the concussion is a helpful tool in the management of the injury (see Cantu below) and depends on: 1) Presence or absence of loss of consciousness, 2) Duration of loss of consciousness, 3) Duration of posttraumatic memory loss, and 4) Persistence of symptoms, including headache, dizziness, lack of concentration, etc.

Coma

The word coma refers to a state of unconsciousness. The unconscious state has variability and may be very deep, where no amount of stimulation will cause the person to respond or, in other cases, a person who is in a coma may move, make noise, or respond to pain but is unable to obey simple, one-step commands, such as "hold up two fingers," or "stick out your tongue." The process of recovery from coma is a continuum along which a person gradually regains consciousness.

For people who sustain severe injury to the brain and are comatose, recovery is variable. The more severe the injury, the more likely the result will include permanent impairment.

End of Careers as a result of Injuries

1. *Daunte Culpepper – Minnesota Vikings*

Vikings fans had reason to celebrate after Daunte Culpepper had a breakout season in 2004. Unfortunately, that celebration quickly turned sour when in 2005 Culpepper injured his knee in a game against the Carolina Panthers. Culpepper was put on the injured reserve list and then released by the Viking in 2006. The Miami Dolphins attempted to give Daunte Culpepper another chance, but he never got back to pre-injury form. During his last four years in the NFL Culpepper played in just 24 games.

2. *Joe Theismann – Washington Redskins*

An 11 year career in the NFL is a lifetime for many players, but Joe Theismann could have kept playing had it not been for a brutal break to his leg. The two-time Super Bowl champion was playing in a Monday night game in 1985 when he suffered a brutal break in both bones on his lower right leg. Thiesmann's career ended courtesy of not one but two linebackers, Lawrence Taylor and Harry Carson. Theismann never stepped out to play on an NFL field again.

3. *Sterling Sharpe – Green Bay Packers*

After six seasons in the NFL Sterling Sharpe was doing everything right. He was a great receiver with soft hands, speed, agility, and the smarts for the game. Unfortunately in 1994 Sharpe was hit and suffered a neck injury that ended his career. A Hall of Fame career sidelined by a single hit only goes to highlight the ferocity of the NFL.

4. *Michael Irvin – Dallas Cowboys*

During his 11-year career in the NFL Dallas Cowboys wide receiver Michael Irving ruled the game. He was flashy, he was fast, and his hands seemed to feature superglue for super feats of catching. In 1999 Irving was playing against the Philadelphia Eagles when he was rushed by Tim Hauck. Irvine actually saw Hauck coming but ducked to avoid a collision and instead hit his helmet on the turf at Philadelphia's Veteran's Stadium.

5. *Darryl Stingley – New England Patriots*

Darryl Stingley only managed four years in the NFL before his time with the New England Patriots and the National Football League came to a sudden end. In 1978 Stingley was involved in a bad collision with Raiders defensive back Jack Tatum. That collision left him with a compressed spinal cord and two broken vertebrae. While he managed to regain limited movement in his arms, he spent the rest of his life in a wheelchair and died in 2007 from complications associated with his condition.

Conclusion

NFL Football is known for it's fascinating highlights and histories, and also for how dangerous the game is. Many teenagers play the sport and as a result of the forces generated, as well as the mismatch in body sizes, incur all kinds of injuries. But the highest injury rates are in professional football.

10

DON'T LOOK BACK

You don't walk away from football, without football going with you. There are **consequences** to playing the game of football.

When I quit my senior year in high school, I did so with a torn ACL the doctors could not repair, and a badly injured right wrist. I also had a myriad of other injuries including cartilage floating around in my other knee, plus neck and back pain, etc., etc.

Not many years after graduating I had surgery on my left knee when loose cartilage got caught in the joint and made my knee lock up. That was the beginning of 17 total knee surgeries over the years. With both knees in deteriorating condition I had to walk with my hips. Swinging my legs like a drunk in an old TV western.

Fortunately, technology finally caught up and I got my torn ligaments replaced. Right knee, with a graft from a donor Achilles tendon flown across the country on dry ice. Left knee, with a strip from my own hamstring. But the surgeries did not replace the cartilage in either knee so the benefit was limited. Finally, joint replacement technology improved and I had bilateral knee replacement surgery.

A relative who saw this type of surgery said it's extremely violent. After the joint is cut open, the ends of the bones are sawed off with a jigsaw. The new metal replacement parts are then hammered into position, so the shaft on the end of the metal bone caps is driven down into the bones with everything fitting perfectly. What got my nephew was how the doctors would rare back and hammer like hell, to get the metal shaft down into the ends of the four sawed-off upper and lower leg bones!

Bilateral knee replacement means both knees. I did mine at one time and came out with 72-metal staples in my legs. I had my morphine drip pump quit in the first 12-hours after surgery. Then again, in the next 12-hours. And that, my friends, was PAINFUL. I kept telling the nurses they had to give me some other pain medicine. They kept saying not without the doctor's permission.

When they couldn't locate the doctor I said, "You have to give me something!" They wouldn't do it, and couldn't get another morphine pump because they were all in use.

My second night in the hospital I convinced a nurse to help me get out of that wicked place. She said I first had to get off the morphine pump. Which I had been forced to do twice with no pain medication to replace it. Plus I'd have to go pills-only for 8-hours or so. I told her, get me the pills and turn off the morphine. This was just after the first 24-hours from my bilateral knee surgeries. I also had to be evaluated by the physical therapist before I could be discharged.

By the time the physical therapist showed the next day, more than 8-hours from getting off the morphine in the middle of the night. I was sitting at my bedside holding the IV rig beside me, waiting for him. He walked in, looked stunned at seeing me seated and fully dressed like I was leaving soon, said hi then just stood there.

Shaking his head he asked, "Did someone help you get your shoes on?"

No, I said. I did it myself. He walked over knelt down and started tying my shoes. While he was tying them I asked, "How do I rate for coming back from bilateral knee replacement surgery?"

He stopped tying my shoe, looked up and said, "In the TOP 1%."

My room was adjacent to the nurse station on that floor. Walking out on my newly hammered-in-place knees early on the second day after surgery. I about scared the nurses to death. They all jumped and started saying,

"Sir! O sir! You shouldn't be walking!"

Then the physical therapist came out behind me and they calmed down. We went to the stairwell to see if I could walk down the steps and back up. On sawed off knees that were replaced with cobalt chromium parts 36-hours before. I passed all the tests and got the nurses to discharge me. Went home skipping two-weeks of rehab in a recovery facility and survived on high doses of Oxycontin and a very strong will and high pain threshold.

My wrist injury lingered after football too. It got bent back badly and was almost useless the last couple games of my injury-plagued last season. But the trainers bandaged me up and I kept playing. The only way to really fix it, doc said, was to take three small bones out and I was tired of it hurting all the time, so...

It was the only surgery I remember waking up while they were operating on me. My eyes just opened. And I noticed the whole room start to sway to the side, then stop rocking slowly... I was staring at the ceiling. The room shook like that again then rocked slowly to a stop. I heard voices and turned to see two doctors by my right hand. Right when one guy took some medical pliers, and with two hands got a hold of a bone in my wrist and started yanking. Like he was trying to pull it out of my body. The whole room swayed again as I was looking sideways.

He was pulling the bones out of my wrist while I watched. When they saw me, the other guy rushed over and gave me more anesthesia. The doctors slit the back of my hand and arm with a 6-inch long incision, far more than necessary. When I woke up I was so drugged I couldn't think right. But I could sure as hell feel the pain in my wrist like they hadn't given me any pain meds. The nurse came in to check me, and I pointed to my forearm hanging from a hook to keep my hand elevated above my heart.

"It hurts right here! Right here!" I said emphatically. "I need something to stop the pain right here!" Sometime later I awoke to see my then-wife had come by to check on me. I said hi, then started pointing somewhere else and saying, "It hurts right here. Right here! Please help! Right here. Help me..."

She looked where I was pointing, figured out what I meant and said, "I can't do THAT in here! You're crazy!"

I waited 10-years after my surgeon said I had three choices, and the third was to live with the pain. Which I chose over the other surgery options. When I met him again years later before my surgery, he asked why I waited so long? I said, he'd given me three options and the last was to live with the pain, so I had been living with the pain.

The doc gave me an incredulous look... Then said, "I was kidding!"

But the worst injury I carried with me, the worst part of football that walked out with me when I walked away from football, was my hate for Coach and how he treated me. I would try to forgive him, but I hated him so it never worked. And a deep-seated inner rage remained buried inside me. A true hatred for his abuse and what it cost me.

Those dark memories lived on in my heart and soul and mind. I could never completely get away from what Coach did to me. I didn't want to. I wanted to HATE IT. He violated so many players. You had to comply and go along with his abusive obnoxious style if you played for him, or else...

Nobody would stand up to him. But I tried to. I stood up to him in my own way. He was wrong. He was violating young talents under his authority, and his targeted abuse to me left a major open wound inside me.

No sutures could patch it. No bandage could help it. There was no way to get down to where it was. My deepest wound from playing football. No doctor had the tools. No therapist could make it go away. No drug could do more than mask it. No amount of liquor ever changed it. You live a life of treating glaring, often obnoxious symptoms. With no hope of figuring out how to really forgive so you can be healed.

Forgive my ex-wives for whatever they did to torment me, I was probably hard to live with. I didn't hate them, but they had to live with my hate too. And let's not forget my kids. Yea, the kids I was abusive to sometimes, from that inner place of rage and fury no one could heal. No one could understand, though I knew exactly where it was coming from. I hated somebody. Really hated them.

Even after Coach died I hated him for what he did to me, cheating me of my greatest opportunities in football. And what he did to that kid, grabbing him by the facemask and pounding his head into the ground. That jerk dishonored so many young men.

I heard once, Coach had become a defensive line coach at the college level. Where he tried grabbing some 300-pound lineman's facemask, and that didn't go so well. The guy decked him. Man I loved hearing that story. Wished I could hear more stories just like it. But living with hate isn't worth it. Hate will contaminate other areas of your life. I lived with it too long. At times I was a bad friend to good friends. A bad father to good kids. Not always, no, because most of the time I was a great guy. But I came with a temper rooted and grounded in hatred.

So, I was a minefield too. Any step and I could be too intense for anybody, including myself. I apologize to my friends. I apologized to my children in tears.

My own life is proof there are consequences to playing the game of football.

But truth be told, I got off lucky compared to many. I only had to live with HATE. Bad is my malady was from football, way too many kids who played have ended up suffering on a much greater scale later in life. Those around them suffering on a greater scale too. Yes, because I'm still alive and kicking, with mind-enough to write this book. My sufferings were nothing compared to the guys who ended up with consequences from head trauma.

Because here's how that shakes out ultimately:

1) The MIND shuts down and the body shuts down with it. So the former player dies with heirs left to grieve for him, or...

2) The MIND shuts down and the body lives on. The former player survives in a debilitated or comatose state, with family members tending to his body till it shuts down completely.

For the wives and children, friends and people in the networks of business associates, church members and so on. Both men are as good as dead, and one is dead. How do you heal that? Sounds like PRE-EMPTIVE actions are needed in advance to prevent this kind of thing in the future of football.

Of course, this was my query regarding my own consequences of playing football. How do I heal that? The HATE inside me? There was no door I could ever find. No key, if there was a door. No way out but to live with it. I kept begging God to help me not-hate anymore! I didn't want to hate. I would plead: "Help me please! Take these memories away. Take this hate out of me. Give me a new mind!"

Then one day something beautiful happened.

It was at the end of the day. I got my pajamas on and went to bed, and lo and behold... I was about to deal with my hate once and for all.

In a dream that night, I'm not sure where I was, but it seemed high up someplace. It was very bright and light was everywhere, I remember that. And I was looking down on Coach and me. We were below where I was watching from, having a conversation in a bright room with no walls. He had already died, but in my dream he was alive.

We were talking with each other, I could see. But I couldn't hear a word we said. My vantage point moved about as time passed. Like a fly on the wall that wasn't there, I saw us walking in this bright white light together, talking. And there was nothing like Anxiety, or Anger or Hate. But something more like Peace.

Actually, looking back... I think it was love.

When I woke up, I didn't hate Coach anymore. I understood. It was okay.

With that miracle and my second divorce, I began to remember the hip, fun, extraordinary man and athlete I really was, and still am. I've been making positive life changes since, and recovering on the inside. No excuses. Time to grow. Time to run a new race. Time to love and give what I can. To everything there is a season. And this season is a time of restoration for me. Reclaiming the better man. Forging myself into a better neighbor and friend.

It took a lot of soul-searching to face writing this book, and especially a couple chapters that brought the bad memories back. Tears had to be shed. But I kept working at it. Didn't give up. Felt like I was playing football again sometimes, the way I had to wrestle with it. The way it opened the burning furnaces in my soul. But I needed to face it so I could share the healing.

Point at your own heart. Take one hand and point at your heart.

Now say: "It all starts right here!"

The men at the top of the game must start taking more personal responsibility for their inactions as much as their actions. The NFL must face reality and stop wimping around with attorneys posturing to save face. A culture of violence is in place without sufficient guidance for the players going back to their youth.

Punt, Pass and Kick competitions are not enough.

Look NFL honchos, you're getting called on the carpet here. Along comes your opportunity to be classy, and be a class act. With athletes facing charges of domestic violence and more… What do you do? What is your response? Send a commissioner out to embarrass you by exposing you. When I heard him say everything would be fully addressed "by the Super Bowl," I laughed out loud.

Calling Mr. Commissioner, are you there? Owners hiding behind Mr. Commissioner… Ring, ring, ring… Anyone there?

Things haven't been handled right, and need to be handled better. For one, a strongly supported POSITIVE CULTURE needs to be developed and managed. Starting in youth sports programs for kids learning the game. The NFL needs to actively help "create and initiate" programs that connect the league to every youth football program in the nation. Where the NFL can provide information to coaches and players of all youth football programs on a monthly basis. Like sending a monthly online magazine that teaches the NFL ethic and code of honor to both players and COACHES.

More than the "weak interface" the NFL now provides online. Something far more interactive that young ballplayers could connect to and interact with on their own.

This would be an excellent way to reach kids and their coaches with the right messages preemptively! To intentionally TRY to connect to the young players as they grow up and continue playing football. Helping them learn the culture the NFL preaches. The nuts and bolts of the basic inner constitution a young boy needs, to become a MAN: Approved by the National Football League.

The USA Football SAFESPORT is in the right direction. But look at the webpage. Yes, if you search it patiently you can see they're covering all the major things they need to. But the format is not user-friendly. Our world is not becoming more ethically self-conscious and responsible, and it never will by itself. If athletes are taught a higher code of honor and ethics from childhood in youth programs supported by the NFL, then the league leadership will have a stronger place, where they can come down hard on players who violate NFL standards for misconduct.

And not to overstate this or pin the tail on the donkey more than deserved, but what about how the LEAGUE is handling the real and true tragedies "Head Trauma" causes? I'm disappointed, but I get it. Money rules. Or does it? Maybe social mores rule in this case, not money. What will it take, for owners to divert their attention from the bottom line to seriously look at more effective options to really make the game safer?

In ways that count!

No wooden-nickel cop-out solutions please. I'm talking about real world remedies. For instance, other major sports are doing more already. Why not form a committee that includes players, coaches and owners together. To evaluate what other major sports are already doing that seems to work for them.

Things like a Penalty Box in hockey, where an amped-up player goes out of a game for some period of time, but is allowed to come back later. Things like Flagrant Technical Fouls in the NBA, where there are degrees of the foul the referees can call at the time of the infraction in games, plus league reviews after the game, plus total infraction counts that bring consequences if a limit is exceeded in a season. New deterrents that work, that players respond to, **that help them keep their aggression in check.**

And how about a quicker whistle or revised rule for when a runner is held up in a pile, and defenders are still running in and hitting the stationary pile. Why not make it where they can't do that anymore. Bring in a penalty box consequence for some things, a flagrant technical foul concept for other situations, and MAKE THE GAME SAFER. Or like FIFA has initiated in pro soccer: the Yellow Card, to give a player a serious warning. Two yellow cards = 1-red card: You're out of the game.

Protect this great game, and the players playing it. Starting by admitting your own culpability. Is it right to hit a woman? No! Is it right to spit in a man's face? No! Is it right to over-punish a child? No! Is it right to ignore a football culture crying out for direction and guidance and fairly enforced standards?

My life was changed by the healing I experienced in a dream. I would love to see that healing designed into the system from youth competitions to the pros in the future. More must be done to change the culture from the bottom up. A group of former and current NFL players, coaches and league officials needs to be formed to revamp, revise and renew how the NFL handles the violence-related issues at the core of a very violent game, going all the way down the line to interactive connection with young players and their coaches.

It's a kid's game first so start there.

How can the NFL become more involved in instilling the ethics of higher principles and standards so kids playing in youth leagues around the country learn the right way to play the game of life, as they learn the violent game of football? The High School Player Development, HSPD concept is in the right direction, based on **5-day camps** held between May and August each year.

Keep going from there.

Expand the connection to high school players to **52-weeks a year** by using existing technology to deliver the messages of ethics and honor in a very user-friendly, fun and interesting weekly format. How can you do the same at every level of the game? Professionally, how can you create a real camaraderie among all players from all teams in the league to be part of this example as NFL stars?

Try to, that's how. Try to accomplish it. Do more.

The Future of Football hangs in the balance. Part on the field, part in the courtroom, part at the sports bar and part in living rooms of fans across the country...

Here it comes like it or not.

Will it be like I've been making the case for? With more multi-threat players taking snaps and sharing the quarterback role? In a "QB Unit" concept...

Maybe... I've seen versions of it in the college game.

Or will drop back pocket passers run the new theory off the field? I know the greatest pocket passers share a critical DRIVE and WILL component. Combined with their leadership skills, that alone makes them more than one-dimensional. I may have overstated my case. I guess we will have to see what unfolds in the future.

If I haven't been fair to anyone in this book, it wasn't meant to be judgmental or cruel. We're all imperfect. So, take it with a grain of salt on your popcorn. Order a drink or two for your entourage, and sit back and enjoy the future of football whether you're jumping up in your seat at an NFL stadium, or leaping off your couch and spilling your beer as an armchair quarterback. The best of the best is yet to come. More entertaining football than ever before. New innovations. New strategies. New rules.

Thank you NFL for the privilege of poking fun at you and acting like I know all the answers when I don't. I do care about this game I love. And I care about the players paying a price to give us something to enjoy at their expense. I wish you well in fielding a safer NFL game for the gladiators putting their lives on the line to play such an entertaining sport for us.

Thank you football fans for taking time to look into the crystal ball with me to see what's trending in football these days. To peer just ahead with a little excitement and expectation, as the epic struggle at the helm continues…

OUTRO

The Dez Bryant Rule – Dez is asked to help NFL rule makers redefine what a catch is. The commissioner sends Bryant a text and asks to meet with him to learn what a catch is. The meeting could double as an autograph-signing / photo-op gig.

Bryant could say, "Here, watch this catch I made to almost win the game against Green Bay, and I'll show you what a catch is."

It was fourth down when Tony Romo took the snap, stepped back and let fly the ball Bryant would leap high into the air to grab with two hands. Two big hands, because Bryant's hands are bigger than the hands of any NFL rule makers.

Flying through the air he lands left foot, then right foot. Drags the left foot again on the turf as he falls taking his third step. While at the same time, switching the ball from both hands to one and reaching the ball out for the goal line.

Which, at that point, was not athletic enough to be a catch for the referees?

In the minds of the officials who weighed the catch on review it wasn't a catch? Though it reminded me of my incredible interception flying out of bounds after leaping high up in the air to steal the pass and seal the win for my team. But no…

Mine was a catch in high school. But Bryant's was incomplete in the pros. How can it be, this sensational play was not considered a catch? Because the refs interpreted the last part of the play was not-athletic-enough to be considered an athletic move? Really now.

Before Bryant reached the ball for the goal and bobbled it on impact, he had taken possession to the point he could switch the ball from two hands to one. He had taken three steps with the ball securely in his control. The Dez Bryant Rule should be simple. It's a video rule. Watch the replays, of one of the most spectacular catches in the 2015 playoffs. To be scrubbed and wiped away by referees who knew some rule that allowed them to claim the last part of the play was not athletic enough to be considered an athletic move.

I'm shaking my head and thinking, what "a reach" that ruling was.

At least there is no question about it. Dez should get the rule changed on his terms. They owe him that much for denying him such an incredibly entertaining spectacle of a catch, and near score for the win!

Or, did he score?

Bryant could say, "Here, watch this touchdown I made, on replay, and I'll show you what a catch, a fumble, a fumble recovery and a touchdown are."

Because in high school, I know the replays show what would have been a touchdown when I played. I saw it more than once myself. My team did it on purpose. Can't get in the end zone on fourth down close to the goal? Fumble on purpose and go for broke. Make your own luck. Recover and score.

But the referees, with their own eyes and replay reviews. Could not collectively realize what any high school ballplayer would know not to call an "incompletion." Like Dez said, "It was a catch."

The Spectacular Rule – If a spectacular play is involved, the refs have to give it special review, where the league can have maybe a group of high school football players given a 51% majority vote on what the final call should be.

The Out of Play / Out of Mind Rule – This would forever solve the problem of making fans watch the ball fly through the air and out of bounds for nothing. There it goes, everybody watch! Look at that distance! Over the goal line, over the back of the end zone and… Out of bounds!

Alternate title: The Most Un-Spectacular Play Rule.

You'd have to be out of your mind to think fans "enjoy" watching that play called a kickoff. It's not a kickoff, it's a KICKOUT. And nobody would rather watch that over getting to see a runback by a speedster kick returner. I think it's a sign we're all getting dementia when I see that on TV. Knowing everybody else watching is lost in the same dull moment. Watching the ball fly out of bounds. Like a gear came loose in their brain engine and their mouths are hanging open.

O, how entertaining! There it goes. The referee chases down the loose ball dodging the cables behind the end zone, the cameras and photographers. Very athletically retrieving the ball so the teams can run a play "in bounds" with it.

You don't see this in the NBA. The basketball is never tossed out of bounds to start a game. There's nothing like it in Major League Baseball. The first pitch is never thrown directly out of play on purpose. Nothing like it in the NHL... The puck isn't sent flying out of play to start a game, or a period. But in the NFL they allow teams to kick the ball directly out of play to start a game, a half, or a change possession.

You have to be out of your mind to think that's entertaining to watch. I was a return guy who returned punts and kicks for touchdowns. That was my thing. One of them, anyway... And it was fun. Let a guy make a spectacular return. Or at least try to. That's far more entertaining for fans than watching a football fly a long distance and land out of play.

The Goose & the Gander Rule – What is good for the owners is good for the fans. When the league reaches the point where this comes true, the fans will be happier about supporting their teams.

The owners have been operating by laws created just for their protection. Concerning certain types of "losses" owners and teams could have, related to terror. Laws that protect the owners from claims by fans who would want to recover something for the damage or injury they incurred due to a terrorist event at an NFL game.

Well, what about the fans?

Should we ask Robert Kraft? Or should we ask Jerry Jones? Who should we ask about this? What about the owners making sure the fans supporting them are protected too?

Here's my proposal to the owners… Let me take a gander and see if I can get your goose: Buy insurance policies for the fans. Add the cost to the price of the tickets or concessions. Protect the fans, not just your own ass. Modify the laws if need be, to protect the fans too!

The Repeat Offender Rule – When evidence is discovered that indicates a team has "intentionally" violated NFL rules, or failed to prevent, stop or disallow the intentional violation of NFL rules regarding any responsibility the team has. They get their socks rocked with penalties, fines, suspensions, kicked out of the league at some point.

Any form of not knowing about something the team is responsible for, is not an excuse. If it involves something related to the actual game played on the field, so that what is "league-sanctioned" becomes "unsanctioned," this rule will be enforced with newly defined standards of severity for repeat offenders.

FUMBLEGATE: *The Cover-up*

Prediction: In the future someone will take time to fully research the New England Patriots fumble statistics from 2007 to 2015. During the same period of years Tom Brady was given responsibility for the pressure in the game balls that he asked for.

The truth will get out, as it always does. The Fumblegate story will get covered with the scrutiny it deserves. As will the present cover-up by the NFL, to not investigate what the Wells Report says the league is tasked to investigate.

Page-1 of the report says: The investigation was conducted pursuant to the Policy on Integrity of the Game & Enforcement of Competitive Rules. That Policy provides that *"actual or suspected competitive violations will be thoroughly and promptly investigated."*

Though stated on the first page of the report, the NFL chose only to investigate the single "known" violation committed in the first half of the AFC Championship game when the Patriots were caught playing with illegally under-inflated footballs. But the NFL ignored how the report indicates other "suspected" violations occurred.

Brady was determined guilty of "generally" knowing what was going on, based on facts *from other games during the 2014 season.* Text messages sent around the times of other games were referenced by the NFL in handing down Brady's penalty. Everyone who read the Wells Report knows, the NFL considered "those text messages" related to the deflating scandal. Enough to use them to conclude Brady must have known something about the "inappropriate" things that were going on in the AFC Championship game.

The report says:

> In particular, we have concluded that it is more probable than not that Jim McNally [the Officials Locker Room attendant for the Patriots] and John Yastrzemski [an

*equipment assistant for the Patriots] participated in **a deliberate effort to release air** from Patriots game balls **after the balls were examined by the referee**.*

*Based on the evidence, **it also is our view** it is more probable than not that **Tom Brady** [the quarterback for the Patriots] **was at least generally aware of the inappropriate activities** of McNally and Yastrzemski **involving the release of air from Patriots game balls**.*

Page-4 of the report defines it further:

*In the **weeks and months** before the AFC Championship Game, McNally periodically exchanged text messages with the Patriots equipment assistant primarily responsible for the preparation of the Patriots game balls, John Yastrzemski. In a number of those text messages, McNally and Yastrzemski discussed the air pressure of Patriots game balls, **Tom Brady's unhappiness with the inflation level of Patriots game balls**, Jastremski's plan to provide McNally with a "needle" for use by McNally, and McNally's **requests for "CASH…"***

Let me start with the "weeks and months" comment. Wouldn't the weeks and months before the AFC Championship be considered **"the regular season?"** So the report could have said: During "the regular season" texts related to deflating game balls, (in games against other teams), were exchanged between McNally and Jastremski.

The report also suggests McNally and Jastremski had a "weekly tradition" of deflating the game balls, by more than once using the phrase **"this week."**

Example #1 - Jastremski: Can't wait to give you your needle **this week** :)

Example #2 - Jastremski: I have a big needle for u **this week**

Hello NFL.

These are obvious references of deflating game balls on a "weekly" basis during the months and weeks before the AFC Championship. These text messages are EVIDENCE of the high probability there was "weekly" cheating during the regular season in other games.

How can this EVIDENCE of cheating in other games be used to condemn Brady in a totally different game, but not be worthy of investigating further regarding "the other games" the texts were being exchanged about? The report identifies a minimum standard of duty the league is obligated to uphold...

"Suspected competitive violations will be thoroughly and promptly investigated."

So, why have the suspected violations been ignored instead?

There are several popular TV shows about investigators digging for clues to solve cases backwards. One called "Homicide Hunter" is about Joe Kenda from Colorado Springs, where he tells how a crime was reported and the ensuing investigation uncovered pertinent facts that led to the successful arrest and convictions of the guilty parties.

Another program is: Forensic Files. Where the same kind of story is told, of investigators proving who was responsible by careful analysis of **the story the evidence tells**. I've watched these shows and how the investigators work. Where investigators put together the story backward from: 1) The story people tell, plus 2) The story the evidence tells.

The Wells Report investigators uncovered pertinent facts indicating the probability that Brady and the Patriots cheated in other games during the *"weeks and months"* before the AFC Championship. But the NFL has not explored any of those FACTS beyond using them as proof Brady deserves to be punished for *"generally"* knowing of the illegal deflating of game balls in the AFC Championship game.

Since the NFL has failed to investigate any of this. Let's take an investigative look at what the report suggests might have happened...

Text-message evidence links the general time frames of games played against the New York Jets, Chicago Bears, Baltimore Ravens and Cincinnati Bengals… to McNally and Jastremski's participation in the inappropriate deflating of game balls. The report infers more 2014-season games should be investigated. Since the perpetrators referred to their practice of deflating game balls as happening weekly.

Without question, the report indicates it is likely game balls were deflated in more games. Of course, Joe Kenda would have wanted to know the extent of the cheating. Any of the investigators on the Forensic Files would have pursued this too. Examining the evidence to determine what story the evidence was telling.

Once Kenda learned McNally had lied in saying he went straight to the field without stopping on the way, (though security cameras told a different story). Kenda would have known McNally was covering up the truth with a false account.

The Wells Report also considered Tom Brady's claim, of not really knowing who McNally was, to be untrue. In the most gracious manner, the report talks about all of this like something almost untouchable. The tone of the report borders on sounding protective.

But TV investigators would want to know if Brady and the Patriots were illegally deflating game balls for the entire 2014 regular season. Especially with evidence making them believe it was likely that they were. And they would discount what McNally or Brady had to say, since both were caught making what investigators considered to be **less than forthright statements**.

Isn't that what a LIE is?

Kenda would have wanted to know if Brady cheated all season. And next, if Brady had cheated in a prior season or seasons. And the Wells Report has more facts Kenda would have scrutinized. Like how McNally referred to himself as "the Deflator" in May 2014, *AFTER THE 2013/14 SEASON*. A very interesting time reference indeed, since McNally was not talking in the future tense. Like he would become "the Deflator" the next season, when Brady would get caught.

No, his claim of being the Deflator came after the 2013/14 season. Which would have been extremely suspicious to Joe Kenda and the Forensic Files investigators. Indicating the obvious likelihood, if not probability the Deflator earned his self-claimed monicker in that previous season or more previous seasons.

Follow the facts: **What story does the evidence tell?**

The investigators in TV crime shows do their jobs like this. They surmise things from what the evidence tells them, then follow where the evidence leads to the ultimate conclusion. If the Brady story was on those shows, the investigators would have reason to suspect Tom Brady cheated in at least two seasons.

Enter New England's fumble statistics during the 8-years Brady was responsible for the pressure in the game balls. During which same-time-period the Patriots rose from the middle of NFL rankings for fumbles in a season, to dominating that statistical category. **Least fumbles of all NFL teams, 8-years in a row.**

What are the odds?

A normal NFL team with normal NFL fumble stats until 2007. Then, _**after Brady let someone start deflating the game balls to his custom preference,**_ the Patriots abruptly had the fewest fumbles in the entire league. And they continued to have the fewest fumbles for 8-straight years? Really...

2007/08 - Patriots #1 fewest fumbles in the NFL.
2008/09 - Patriots #1 fewest fumbles in the NFL.
2009/10 - Patriots #1 fewest fumbles in the NFL.
2010/11 - Patriots #1 fewest fumbles in the NFL.
2011/12 - Patriots #1 fewest fumbles in the NFL.
2012/13 - Patriots #1 fewest fumbles in the NFL.
2013/14 - Patriots #1 fewest fumbles in the NFL.

2014/15 - Patriots #1 fewest fumbles in the NFL.

Critical math minds are on record for saying this could not be "random fluctuation." Knowing by the forensics of math, that 8-consecutive years of dominating the fewest-fumbles category should be impossible. Since it would be profoundly against the odds.

Joe Kenda would put 2 & 2 together and question the validity of the team's suspect fumble stats. Knowing they happened to match the same time period, 2007 to 2015, when Brady had permission to customize his game balls.

Let the evidence tell its own story.

Take the same math probabilities to Las Vegas, and here's how it works there. The casinos have people watching the gamblers. Anytime one starts winning more than the odds predict. Very simple… It is confirmed. Beating the odds consistently, (more than random fluctuation allows), is not possible. Someone is either "counting cards" or employing some other means to defy the odds.

Casinos consider this against their rules and illegal. Upon discovering the evidence a player is counting cards, the casinos will have them escorted to the door and told they are not welcome to return.

But wait! Where is the evidence to justify kicking them out?

The evidence is in the numbers. The odds… How the results are not consistent with random fluctuation… The gambling world knows nobody really beats the odds and continues to beat them. Casinos know when a player is counting cards. They can't read a player's mind, and card counters never admit to counting cards. Yet, casinos KNOW when its happening. And they kick out the card counters without any hard proof, other than knowing random fluctuation is being defied.

If the casinos were in charge of things in the NFL, they would have recognized the odds-defying pattern of the Patriots unlikely fumble statistics long before 8-years had run its course. They would have KNOWN something was up, something was amiss. Gambling professionals know the Patriots 8-consecutive years of fewest fumbles is a bust based on how, it is too-odds-defying.

If you fall on a pillow, it won't pop out of your arms like a fully inflated football. Same goes for a football that has been illegally deflated. A half inflated football would be twice as easy to hold onto. Any degree of illegal deflation would make a football some-degree easier to hold onto and "not-fumble."

The team with the fewest turnovers WINS! *Almost always...*

New England had the fewest fumbles in the league 8-straight years.

How did they do it?

This cannot be explained away as anything normal. The Patriots fumble stats from 2007 through 2015 are suspect by the forensics of MATH. One team accomplishing such statistical dominances in a single category would be EXTREMELY ABNORMAL for so many years.

What is a reasonable explanation? Other than the known deflation of game balls to Brady's thinner preference? Because it appears the Patriots may have been cheating on a **weekly basis** the past 2-seasons. Which would lead any intelligent investigator to at least question if the team might have cheated more than 2-years... Since no other plausible reason has been offered to explain the inexplicable fumble statistics.

Rigging the game to where your team has fewer turnovers because they play with under-inflated footballs is cheating. Doing it in 128-regular season games, not to mention playoff games, would eclipse the cheating scandal of The Postal Service cycling team in the Tour de France.

But what if it was partly accidental, unintended and unknown?

What if no other Patriots realized Brady was letting *"someone he didn't know"* custom-deflate his game balls to an illegally under-inflated psi pressure? So the running backs didn't know they were running with under-inflated balls, during the 8-years Brady"s request to handle Patriots game balls was permitted by the league. And what if the coach didn't know and neither did the owner?

Oh my! What a messy situation for a commissioner with the responsibility to investigate "suspected" violations THOROUGHLY... Yes, what a mess it would be for the NFL to acknowledge how the investigators on crime-solving TV shows would think more cheating had occurred.

Based on the evidence from the Wells Report and the forensics of math...we KNOW the Patriots were doing "something" to achieve such improbable results... Something tangible that should be identifiable.

"Something" ...that gave them better odds of winning against every team they played the past **128**-regular season games since 2007.

"Something" ...that allowed them to "impossibly" dominate NFL fumble statistics with fewer fumble turnovers than any other team for 8-straight years.

"Something" ...apparently no other NFL team was doing.

Was it some kind of new gloves their runners were wearing? That made it easier to not-fumble the ball. Was it something the coach said to the ball carriers to make them hang onto the ball better?

What was it?

What were the Patriots doing, the same 8-years Brady's game balls were being deflated to his "less-pressure" preference by a phantom Brady didn't even know?

The TV investigators and the Vegas guys who bust card-counters would probably agree: The Pats beyond-realistic fumble stats, at least "could be" due to softer game balls deflated below NFL standards. Deflated to where they were easier to hold onto and not fumble. Without another clue to follow to suggest it was something else, TV investigators would have investigated the possible connection between Tom Brady customizing his game balls for

8-years, to his team having the fewest fumbles in the NFL for the exact same 8-years.

Come on, folks. Run the numbers.

Here's another clue to follow. Probably the easiest way to prove whether the Pats were cheating for 8-years, or not. Pay attention to the 2015/16 NFL season... And wait till the statisticians run all the numbers so everybody can see the results... And see if the Patriots suddenly fail to lead the league in fewest-fumbles for a 9th-straight year... Yea, because if they don't, then everyone will KNOW the team's fumble statistics were probably connected to the Deflategate scandal.

How can people not-suspect illegally deflated balls were the cause for the unexplainable Patriot fumble stats, if the Pats can't maintain their fumble-stats dominance when everyone KNOWS they are playing with fully inflated footballs in the 2015/16 regular season?

I believe the Patriots will NOT maintain their profound fumble stats dominance a 9th-consecutive year. But will return to normal fumble statistics, like before the league granted Brady's request to let the teams be responsible for their own game balls.

In my opinion, there is enough proof to all but know Brady's game balls were getting deflated below NFL limits during their odds-defying 8-year advantage they maintained in the **128-games** played between 2007 and 2015.

As a former lead crime reporter for the Delaware and Maryland State News, I see the whole debacle through the eyes of an investigative reporter. Who keeps asking questions and pursuing leads. Let others deal with the actual guilt of any guilty parties. I'm giving you the reasons why I think there will be a book written about this topic in the future. That carefully, from in-depth research and analysis, lays out the story the evidence tells.

I do NOT believe Tom Brady waited to start lowering the pressure in his game balls when the NFL granted his request to do so. Once the league gave him permission, I believe Brady had "someone" lowering the pressure